WHAT JESUS DID

What Jesus Did

THEODORE PARKER FERRIS

NEW YORK

OXFORD UNIVERSITY PRESS

1963

Contents

WHAT JESUS DID

INTRODUCTION

ONE OF THE THINGS that I hope to do in the pages that follow is to introduce the reader to a person he already knows about, but whom he may never have met personally. I refer to Jesus of Nazareth.

I have two reasons for wanting to do this. The first is that I want as many people as possible to meet and know Jesus, both for their sake and for his. The second you might call an ulterior reason. I want people to know more about him so that they will have something to stand on when they begin to think and talk about Jesus, especially about who he was.

People who think at all about the Lord Jesus sooner or later begin to wonder who he was, where he came from, and how he is related to the ultimate nature of things. The Church says that he was a man in whom the fullness of the Godhead visibly dwelt, that he was God incarnate in human life, that he was the Word of God made flesh, that he was the Son of God. This is difficult for many people to take in, especially if they know virtually nothing about the theological language of the third and fourth centuries in which the Church stated its belief about Jesus; and even more especially if they know next to nothing about Jesus himself, what he said, what he did, and what it was about him that led people to think of him in terms of the infinite and divine.

Many Americans believe that Abraham Lincoln was the Great Emancipator and some go so far as to believe that he was the very incarnation of the American Spirit. But there are other Americans who believe neither of these things about Lincoln, and the only way that you will ever know where you stand is to look at Lincoln himself, see what he did, read what he said, know the kind of person he was, feel the impression he made upon his contemporaries, and then draw your own conclusion.

The approach to Jesus, though on a different plane, is essentially the same. Not until you know something about him are you in a position to agree or disagree with what the Church says about him. You cannot say that you do not believe in the divinity of Christ until you know enough about him to give you good reason for saying it. Unfortunately, most of the people in the churches who go about saying that they think that Jesus was a great and good man but that they cannot believe that he was divine, are in no such favorable position. They have the general idea that no man can be God; their common sense tells them that, and up to a point, they are right. But what it is about this particular Man that induced people to think of him in such an unusual way they do not often know.

In so small a book as this I have concentrated upon what Jesus did and have referred only incidentally to what he said. I realized that the Sermon on the Mount, to say nothing of the Parables, called for a book of its own, a book written by someone with far greater technical knowledge of the material than I possess. What he said, the human race is not likely soon to forget, but it is what he did that reaches the hearts of people and gives to what he said an authority and meaning which the words by themselves would not have.

I have made no attempt to conceal my own conclusions about Jesus, nor have I tried to press them upon the reader. What I have tried to do is to reveal him as far as it is possible for one person, with his imperfect understanding and limited vision, to reveal another.

Needless to say, not everything that Jesus did is included in this brief account. I have chosen the things which seem to me to be the most significant, and without which no picture of Jesus is complete. Following the Gospel narrative, I have given more time and attention to the way he died than to any other single thing that he did.

What I have written was originally spoken, and the spoken word is quite different from the written word. I am well aware of the hazards involved in switching from one to the other, but I know that there are times when something written to be read can be spoken with great power and effectiveness, and I hope that there may also be times when what was originally spoken may be read without losing all of its effectiveness.

Before we begin, let me sharpen the focus upon our subject. I said at the beginning that one of the purposes of this book is to give the reader more knowledge of Jesus than he already has so that he will stand on firmer ground when he faces the question, What think ye of Christ?

But this book is not an exercise in knowledge, not even theological knowledge. If it may be called an exercise at all, it is an exercise in devotion. Indeed, I hope that it will help people think about Jesus more clearly and accurately; but far beyond that is my hope that it will draw a few people closer to him. After all is said and done, the Christians who have made the greatest contribution to the world are not the ones who have thought most correctly about Jesus, but the ones who have loved him most. To be sure, when the love is supported by sound thinking so much the greater is its power. But the soundest thinking in the world, without the love, will move neither mountains nor men.

The people I am looking for are not the people who say right off what they do or do not believe about Jesus, the people who know all the answers and who are ready to say at the drop of a hat that we are living in a post-Christian world. I am looking for the people who are open to the wonder of him who is like no other. I am interested not so much in what they say as in what they do when they see him. I care not so much about the language of their creeds as I do about the quality of their deeds.

William Mitchell, the Quaker schoolteacher and father of Maria Mitchell, the distinguished astronomer, said to one of his pupils early in the nineteenth century, "Thee must wonder; thee must watch closely; then thee will see and know for thyself."

So I say to you as we now turn toward Jesus: You must wonder; you must watch closely; and then you will see and know for yourself.

I

HE *performed miracles*

WHEN WE BEGIN to think of the things that Jesus did, we are almost certain to think first of the unusual things that he did, things that people ordinarily cannot and do not do. Take a passage like this, for example. "Now when the sun was setting, all they that had any sick brought them unto him; and he laid his hands on every one of them, and healed them." That is unusual. Ordinary people cannot and do not do that sort of thing. But that is not all. The record goes on to say that on more than one occasion he multiplied food, that he stopped a storm, that he walked on the water, that he changed water into wine, and that he even raised the dead. These unusual things that Jesus did are usually referred to as "miracles."

It is a strange and interesting fact that for centuries it was these very miracles which drew people to Christ. They believed in him precisely because he did things that they could not do. They were drawn to him by what they believed were his supernatural powers. Now, in our scientifically oriented civilization, the miracles are more likely to keep people away from him; they are barriers for many a serious-minded person. Instead of substantiating him, they alienate him from people. For many people they wrap him in a smoke screen of fantasy.

And even more interesting and strange is the fact that our attitude toward miracles is in many ways ambivalent. On the one hand, with our scientific sophistication we are suspicious of them when we read about them in the lives of other people; when we meet them we are inclined to discount them and, if possible, sweep them under the carpet. On the other hand, we are looking for them all the time in our own lives as short cuts to health and prosperity — and when we find the drugs that do things that we thought were impossible, we call them the "miracle drugs."

One thing we know before we go far in the company of Jesus is that we must come to some kind of terms with these unusual things he did. Otherwise we will be blocked on every page of the New Testament; we will be bewildered by everything we hear about Jesus. We will be thrown off the track again and again until we know what we think about the miraculous stories that appear on almost every page of the Gospels. Did he do them or didn't he? If he did, what difference does it make? Do similar things happen now?

These are some of the questions which every person must answer for himself. I cannot answer them for you, and I do not intend to. I shall, however, make four simple statements of fact which may help you to answer them. They are all statements that are well within your range of experience; and the first two of them, at least, are extremely obvious.

The first is this. *Extraordinary people do extraordinary things.* Mozart wrote a concerto when he was five years old. Most people do not. St. Francis could preach to the birds and hold their attention. Most people cannot. Dr. Trudeau, a victim of tuberculosis, went to the Adirondacks to die, and found in that very place a cure for the disease that was killing him. Most people just die.

It is not to be wondered at, therefore, that Jesus did extraordinary things for he was, to say the very least, an extraordinary person. There is much more that you can say about him than that, but that is the least you can say. The depth of his inner life — what man would ever dare to plumb it? The intensity of his dedication — who would ever dare to measure it? And is it not true that a man whose inner life is both intense and deep is almost bound to do things that to the less gifted seem to be miraculous in the sense that they are beyond their power of prediction and performance? And when this man happens to be the Incarnate Son of God, it is not surprising that he did unusual things. That is the first fact about the miracles to keep in mind. He who was an extraordinary person did extraordinary things.

The second statement is, *The more extraordinary the person is the more people are inclined to exaggerate the stories about the things he does.* Every well-informed person knows that Mahatma Gandhi did incredible things, things beyond anyone's imagining. He had an influence over the masses of India which no one thought that anyone could ever have, and that no one has ever had since. But the stories that devoted followers told about the things that Gandhi did, including healing the sick and raising the dead, were so excessive in their extravagance that he himself had to deny them publicly.

We are prepared, therefore, for a certain amount of exaggeration in the stories about the things that Jesus did.
For example, in the story of the feeding of the five thousand, it is altogether possible that as the story was told from
generation to generation (and told, mind you, by people
who adored him, and who were telling it because they
adored him) it is altogether possible that the number of
people fed grew larger and larger and the amount of food
on hand grew smaller and smaller. The thing to notice is
that the exaggeration is itself a precious bit of evidence
of how people felt about him and tells us more about him
than all the figures, no matter how accurate they might
have been, that a Bureau of Statistics might have reported.
In their eyes, he was the one who could do anything, the
one who was equal to any emergency. He could make a
little go a long way, he could stretch their meager resources
to incredible lengths. And is it any wonder that in their
memory he *did* do everything?

The third statement is this. *All the extraordinary things
that Jesus is reported in the Gospels to have done are also
reported to have been done by other men both in the Old
Testament and in the New Testament.* Joshua made the
sun stand still. Elijah multiplied food and ascended into
heaven in a whirlwind. Elisha raised a boy from the dead.
Peter and John healed a lame man. Paul was let out of
prison miraculously, by an angel — the gate opened of its
own accord. And one time when he was preaching in someone's house a young man sitting in an open window went
to sleep, fell out of the window and was killed, and Paul
brought him back to life.

Do you see the point without my making it? The unusual

things that Jesus did, the things that we call the "miracles," are not the ground of our faith in Christ as the Incarnate Son of God. If we had no other grounds save the miracles, we would have nothing. They are included in our faith in him, for he was a man of transcendent power in whom God was at work, but what he did others have done before and since, so that the fact that he did these things, even if every one of them could be authenticated, would not in itself be any reason for believing that in him the fullness of the Godhead dwelt bodily.

Dr. William E. Orchard was one of the great preachers of the Congregational Church in England. When I was in the seminary he shook the religious world by becoming a Roman Catholic. He was not only a great preacher but also a profound thinker, and he said one time in reference to the miracles, "If I saw someone walking on the sea, I would not say 'This man is divine.' I would say, 'Excuse me, do you mind doing that again? I didn't see how you did it.' " This statement of Dr. Orchard calls our attention to the fact that it is not the miraculous that reveals the depths of a man's life, and that if we knew nothing of Jesus save the unusual things he did, we would not be following him to-day as our Master and Saviour.

The fourth statement is this. *Especially noticeable about these unusual facts of Jesus is the fact that Jesus never used his power for his own sake.* Not to feed himself when he was hungry, not to save himself when he was dying on the cross, did he ever use the power he undoubtedly had in his own behalf. Nor did he use it, which is even more remarkable, to promote his cause, the Kingdom of God. When he healed a man he urged him not to tell anybody about it.

Of course the man paid no attention to him. He went out and broadcast it by word of mouth to everyone within hearing distance. But he urged him to keep it quiet. He determined at the very beginning of his ministry, if the story of the temptations means anything, that he was not going to dazzle the people into the Kingdom of God. If he could not change their hearts and draw them into it by the power of his love and by the claims of God, then he would let them remain outside.

This we can say without any reservations. If ever a man had at his finger-tips the power that could make both men and nature the servants of his will, Jesus had it. If ever there was a man who used that power carefully and humbly to the point of virtually rejecting it altogether at the end, Jesus was that man.

We cannot leave this subject without bringing it into our own lives and into our own homes, and I shall try to do it in a way in which I am not accustomed to do it, in the first person singular. It is the only way I know how.

I, as a minister of Christ, come into your home. You are sick, in pain. Can I make you well immediately? All I can say is that I never have. There are some, I believe, who can, but I never have. And I have never known anyone personally who was so cured or who effected such a cure. (This is my lack.) Or, your child has died. Can I raise him from the dead and bring him back to life? All I can say is that I never have. I never expect to. Or, you haven't enough food for the next day. Can I go out to the ice-box and multiply the little food that is there? I never have; I never expect to. Or your house is in danger; a hurricane is coming up the coast. Can I stop the storm? All I can say is that I never have, and I have never known anybody who did.

What then can I do? Am I, and all the other ministers of Christ, left helpless with my hands tied behind my back? I do not think so for an instant. I can bring you *him* in a way which is beyond my power of understanding, in a way that is completely dissociated from anything that I am by my own worthiness or virtue; but as a vehicle, as an agent, as a representative of his Body, I can bring him to you. I may not even say anything about him, but I can bring him into your home, he who once did wonders because God was in him, and whose power is now at work in the world. You can accept him. You may not. But you can, not so much because you think he will do something for you, but because you recognize something in him that is so real that you reach out for it to fill the emptiness that you know is in your life.

If you do, then almost anything can happen! Whatever strength you need, bodily, mentally, spiritually, will be given you; perhaps not always instantaneously, but after a long period of pain and anxiety. But it will be given you. The food you need will be provided, one way or another. The storm may not be stopped, but you will have the power to ride it. Your dead may not be raised, but the fear of death in you will be laid completely low forever. And what is more, *you* will be a new man.

All the stories, you see, about the unusual things that Jesus did point only to one thing, namely, to the fact that he himself is the miracle, that in his human life the love of God found a "local habitation and a name," and that through him that love can be communicated to people now, and that power can be radiated in the world of rockets and hydrogen bombs. Never say that it cannot because I have seen it given to people who needed it desperately in emergencies.

He himself is the miracle and the stories about the miracles simply point you and draw you to him, in the hope that you will respond to him positively and affirmatively. His world is different from ours; his way of thinking about the world is quite different from ours. Do not try either to make him into a modern American or to be yourself an ancient Jew. Neither is possible. Take him as he once was and now is, the Life-giver.

This much we know, at least I do, and I can say it without any qualifications at all: I know that wherever and whenever he is now present, unusual things are bound to happen.

II

HE *forgave sins*

WE ARE TRYING to focus our attention upon some of the things Jesus did, the things which make him the Person he is, unmistakable and unlike any other. We are doing this, I hardly need to say, not from a purely academic point of view, and certainly not as an historian would investigate a famous man of another age. We are doing it for a much more personal reason, because we know that we cannot be close to Christ unless we know him. The more we know about him the closer he will be to us and we to him. We are doing it in order to be in more perfect union with him.

In the last chapter we thought about the extraordinary things he did, the things we call the "miracles." Now we turn to something quite different, something which may at first seem easier for us to think about but which is actually much more difficult.

On one occasion Jesus was in a house teaching. He taught very little in the synagogue or the temple because very early in his career he wore out his welcome. He taught, rather, in unconventional places, like the seashore, or someone's house, where large groups gathered. Some of them came simply because they thought he might heal their diseases and some came out of curiosity; others were there for more serious reasons.

In the midst of his teaching some men arrived carrying another man on a stretcher. He was on a stretcher because he couldn't walk; he was paralyzed. They could not get through the crowd that surrounded Jesus, so they went up the outside stairway that every Oriental house has and let the man down through the opening in the roof. At the end of a sentence, or in the middle of one, there was a paralyzed man lying before Jesus.

If you did not know the story, I wonder what you would say might have been the first word Jesus spoke to the man. I should be willing to venture the guess that almost no one would come upon the words that he actually did say. What he said when he saw the man was, "My friend, your sins are forgiven." What sins? We don't know. We know nothing else about the man, and it is presumable that Jesus had never seen him before. The man apparently was a complete stranger to him. Whatever his sins may have been, they were obviously not sins committed against Jesus himself. It was not any snub or injustice done to himself which Jesus was forgiving. It was forgiveness on a larger scale than that.

Jesus did not know what the man's sins were, but he did know that he was a sinner because he was a human being. He knew that it is the tendency of all human beings to turn inward upon themselves, rather than outward, and that as they turn inward, they turn away from God and do things that they would not otherwise do. In this sense, then, he knew that the man was a sinner.

He also knew that sin and sickness often work together

in close partnership. Especially was it so understood by the Jews at that particular time. They had been taught, at least in the popular religious teaching that most of the people were given, that suffering of any kind, whether it be bodily sickness or failure in business, or exile in an alien land, was a sign of God's displeasure. Jesus knew that in the minds of his people sin and sickness were closely associated. They do not always go together but, even today, how often they walk hand in hand with each other, the sickness the outward sign of the inner sin, the sin the consequence of the physical limitation. We perhaps understand this even more clearly than he did, but I am perfectly sure that he knew more about it than many people now give him credit for knowing.

He knew that the man was suffering from paralysis of the body, but he also knew that the man's body might be stiff — *might*, I say — because his conscience was stricken with guilt. At any rate, whatever his sins may have been (and these we will never know), Jesus forgave them. The conservative leaders who were present were shocked, outraged. They said, "Who can forgive sins but God? This man is guilty of blasphemy." While they were arguing back and forth as to the degree of his blasphemy and about what he had done, he, with a characteristic interest in the human element in the situation, turned to the man and said, "Get up, pick up your bed, and go home." And the man did! The record says that when it was all over the people said, "We have seen incredible things today."

One of the things Jesus did while he was alive on earth was to forgive sins, and this is what I ask you to concentrate upon now.

Before we stop to look at the light that this throws upon Jesus, and it throws an enormous amount of light on him, on his nature, and his very being, let us look a moment at ourselves. First of all, let us admit frankly that we do not like the idea of sin. I am using "we" in the sense of a corporate society, we as an American people, we as a good Christian people, living in the twentieth century, molded in our way of thinking and living by the amazing discoveries of science. We do not like the idea of sin.

In the first place, it suggests to many people repression, and repression is anathema. (I wonder how many lives have been ruined by the wrong kind of repression?) It suggests also an unnatural suppression of so many things we so dearly like to do. It implies a limitation of our freedom as human beings and an unfair restriction on our right to make the most of the few brief years that we have on earth, and to go our own way, and to have our own way. It brings to our minds in some cases a thin-lipped, self-righteous old maid sitting in harsh judgment on a young girl who has made a mistake. I wonder if you have that picture tucked away somewhere in your mind.

It also brings to a great many people's minds the picture of a God who sees everything that we do and who thinks that most of the things we do are wrong, especially anything that gives us pleasure, and who takes most of the joy out of life. How terrible it would be to believe in a God like that!

So, by and large, we don't like the idea of sin at all. We like even less to *say* that we have sinned. We admit, with our characteristic American frankness and honesty, that we make mistakes from time to time. This is our own responsibility, our own fault, natural and to be expected in human beings, and may not involve anyone else. And we are quite willing to admit, if we have any understanding of ourselves at all, that we have made such mistakes. But sin is a different thing because sin implies that we are responsible to Someone else. It is not only a mistake that we have made in our checkbook, or a mistake in judgment about our child. It is something that breaks the relationship with Someone infinitely higher than we are; it is a violation of a solemn obligation, and it implies that in the long run we will be called to answer to that responsibility and for that violation, that these things will not simply be forgotten and swept aside, but that they will be a part of us and that we will be called to answer in ways and at a time which we do not now know.

Therefore, we do not often say that we have sinned. Many people who go to church every Sunday do not like to say the General Confession, and when they do say it, they do so only to conform to the pattern of public worship; they do not feel what they say. In fact, they feel that it is humiliating to say that they are "miserable sinners." Perhaps the words are too strong for regular use. You do not and cannot always feel miserable about it. But regardless of how they feel, they do not like to say that they have done something which has violated a supreme relationship and that they will be held responsible for it.

So, we as a people have dropped the word from our vocabulary, except to make fun of it, and we have dropped the idea from our thinking. I say that we have dropped the idea, but the strange thing is that we can't, we really can't drop it, no matter how hard we try. No matter how many people there are who will help us rationalize what we have done, and who will help us find reasons for dropping the idea of sin, we cannot really do it.

There are only two ways, so far as I can see, that you can do it. One is to put your conscience to sleep, to drug it, so that you no longer have any sense of right and wrong. It is as though you demagnetized the needle of a compass so that it no longer pointed to the pole star. That is one way of doing it, and some people have done it rather well. They have reached the point where they can do almost anything, either in private or in public, and not be troubled by it. People who appear respectable can steal the public's money without giving it a passing thought, or tell a lie about another person and never think of it afterward. But most of us can't. If we are normal, healthy people, most of us cannot do it because our conscience is there, and even though we let it slumber, it wakes up at inconvenient times and boldly points us toward the pole star. No, we cannot get rid of the idea of sin that way.

The other way, a more sophisticated way, is to convince yourself that God is in everything and that everything is in God. What I am saying now I wish not to be taken as a criticism of the great Eastern religions because I do not know enough about any of them to make any final judgment. But I know that people who do not live in the East have this idea of God, and I know how beguiling an idea it is. It gives them peace and serenity. God is in the bloom of the flower; he is also in the fading of it. God is in the birth of a baby; he is also in the baby's death from starvation. God is in the love of a man for his wife. He is also in the man's yearning for someone who is not his wife. There's the rub of all monotheism that becomes absolute. It takes away the distinction between right and wrong, for whatever is, is right.

Some people can go that religious way, but most of us cannot. As Westerners we are dipped and dyed in the idea that God is righteous, and however we explain evil, whether we personify it in terms of the devil, or whether we think that is too old-fashioned and therefore speak of it in impersonal terms, we as Westerners are saturated with the idea that there is a difference between right and wrong, that God is eternally righteous, and that when we worship him we reject evil, and that when we sin we commit evil.

So we are left with our sins. We cannot get rid of them. We cannot even get rid of the idea of them, if the truth were known, even the smartest among us.

We turn to Jesus. He spent most of his short life fighting sin, not the sins that the vice squads go out to fight, but the invisible sins of good people; the sin of thinking that you are better than other people; the sin of trying to get the best seat wherever you are, and pushing your way forward regardless of any inconvenience to anyone else; the sin of getting your own way by force, by cruelty, if need be, even by violence, if it is necessary; the sin of putting all your trust in material things, in the stock market, in the things that money can buy; the sin of putting all your trust in these transient things that disappear like the morning dew; the sin of sitting in judgment upon other people when you really never know what the whole story is; the sin of satisfying your own desires at the expense of someone else; the sin of making the House of Prayer a place of business.

I could go on and on. In the few brief months of his

public ministry, Jesus spent a large part of the time fighting sin in the sense that he tried to show people what it
was and give them both the power and the incentive to overcome it. That is the first great fact about Jesus and sin.

The other side of the paradox is that while he fought
the sin he forgave the sinner as he embraced him with his
understanding and love. I have already told you one instance of it. You can remember others in the Gospels. A
woman was being stoned to death according to the Jewish
Law, because she had committed adultery. Jesus came into
the crowd and said, "Let him that is without sin among you
cast the first stone." All the men gradually left the scene.
And he said to the woman, when he was alone with her,
"Hath no man condemned thee?" She said, "No man, Lord."
"Neither do I condemn thee," said Jesus to her.

There are other instances of this in the Gospels, and
they move us almost to tears. But at the end comes the
climax when he forgave the people of the world who killed
him. "Father, forgive them, for they know not what they
do." In this, people ever since have felt the forgiveness of
God.

In no one of these instances could Jesus undo the wrong
that had been done. Once it was done, it was done. He
could not undo it. And in one sense, he could not spare
the person the consequences of what he had done, but he
could do something for the person who did it. He could
accept him, he could take away his guilt, he could restore
his self-respect in the sight of God, he could give him a
new lease on life, and a new incentive to live a life that
was better than the one he had lived.

It goes without saying that he could not do it unless the

person were willing. He could not do it for Pilate or for the Pharisees because they were not ready for it. But he was always willing, and always ready.

In this strange dilemma in which we as human beings live, in which we do things that we know are wrong, and people do things to us that are wrong, we find Jesus most Godlike in the way he resisted sin and yet received sinners like ourselves into his presence.

What I should like you to do now is to sit still, think about yourself in the light of it, and then say aloud, "Lord, be merciful to me a sinner." If you do that, you may hear him say something like this, "My friend, your sins are forgiven."

III

HE *associated with undesirable people*

"AND IT CAME TO PASS, as Jesus sat at meat in the house, behold, many publicans and sinners came and sat down with him and his disciples." The house referred to was Matthew's. Jesus had just asked Matthew to give up a very profitable business of tax-collecting and join him and a little company of non-profit-making teachers, preachers, and healers. Matthew, surprisingly enough, had agreed to do it and responded by asking Jesus and his friends to join him at his house for a meal. Jesus went. He accepted the invitation in spite of the fact that there wasn't one other person present who was what you might call a Jew "in good standing." They were all off the beaten track.

In this book we are making an effort to see more clearly what Jesus did, what it was that made him unique, how he behaved in this strange, mysterious world. Among the things that he did, surely we must include this: he associated with the undesirable people in the community. It sounds so mild when you say it, but his life was cut short largely because of it.

Before we explore this particular phase of Jesus' life, notice how one theme overlaps the other. In the first chapter we began with the miracles, the extraordinary things Jesus did, things that completely pass our understanding. In the last chapter the miraculous healing of a paralytic led to something of far greater significance, namely, the forgiveness of sin. And in this chapter, the dinner at Levi's house — for that was the name he was more popularly known by — reaches back to the idea of sin and leads us on to something even greater.

To see what that is, we must look more carefully at the incident itself. First, who were the "publicans and sinners"? They are something like the Medes and the Persians — they always go together. The publicans were Jews who collected taxes for the Roman government. They were paid agents in the service of the enemy. That was the first count against them. Added to that, they were often rich at the expense of their own people, for they were free to squeeze the pockets of the people, and whatever they managed to get over and above the tax that Rome required they could keep for themselves. They had, therefore, the unique dishonor of being twice cursed. They were collaborators with the enemy, and they were notoriously dishonest with their own people.

The sinners were people who had separated themselves from the religious community, either by breaking one of the laws, such as the law against murder or theft or adultery, or by refusing to accept the strict standard of interpretation of the law that the Pharisees demanded. I thought of them in Nantucket when I read that the Quaker Community, which was the heart of Nantucket in the eighteenth century, thought that it was improper and altogether too worldly for people to have houses built of brick. When in the early years of the nineteenth century prosperity came rolling in with every

tide, some of the people nevertheless built brick houses as
fine as were ever built and were promptly read out of meeting. Because they refused to accept the interpretation of
morality imposed by the community, they became "outsiders." They were comparable to the sinners who were at
Matthew's house with Jesus.

Jesus spent a great deal of time with these people, not because he didn't care about the others, but because no one else
cared about them. They were in a kind of social and religious
quarantine. He made it quite clear that he felt that they
needed him more than the others did. He came the way a
doctor comes, not to the well people, but to the people who
are sick. The publicans and sinners were sick in the sense
that they were cut off from the life of the community like a
limb lopped off a tree.

Jesus did not associate exclusively with these people, people we might call "outsiders." He had many other friends
who lived and worked within the conventional circles of
community life. Simon and Andrew, I am sure, were hard-
working, law-abiding Jews; Nicodemus and Joseph of Ari-
mathea were intellectual, soul-searching Jews, and there
must have been many others. But the impression we get is
that he could not do much for the "righteous," so-called,
the "insiders." They didn't know that they were sick, in soul
if not in body, therefore he could not heal them. Often their
self-righteousness was an impenetrable wall which he could
not break through. Their very goodness was a barrier which
he could not penetrate, for it blinded them both to the fullness of *his* life and to the emptiness of *their own*. Conventional goodness can easily do that. Watch out for it!

It is hard for a good, well-to-do person today to see what

Christianity is about, and to grasp what it means to thousands of people. Such a person has ostensibly everything he needs and, within certain respectable limits, he is doing what he thinks he ought to do. He may even think that he is living by the Golden Rule and have some justification for thinking it. He is like the man of sixty who says, "I've never been ill a day in my life!" That man cannot really appreciate what a doctor means, or what a hospital does, although he may give lavishly to the support of hospitals and medical schools. Unless he has been flat on his back, depending on what a doctor can do to save his life, it is almost impossible for him to appreciate either a doctor or a hospital. If he has never been seriously ill, he does not know what it means to be either sick or well. Very much like him is the conforming American who in the eyes of the community is acceptable and who therefore in his own eyes is about as good as a man can hope to be.

Therefore Jesus came often to the others, not always but often, to the people we call today the "outsiders." There was a chance that he might do something for them, because some of them were aware that they were in need, that they were in trouble, and they wanted what he had to give. They turned to him instinctively, the way a plant turns toward the sun; and he turned to them.

What was their response? According to the Gospels, there were two publicans who responded, Matthew and Zacchaeus; one Roman soldier; one adulteress; one harlot; and one thief; a total of six. Not a very impressive number. Were there any others? We have no way of knowing. We suspect that there were, but knowing people, we also suspect that there were not too many others. We also know that Jesus, unlike

so many of us today, never counted on numbers. When he
chose the men who were to continue his ministry in the
world, how many did he choose? A thousand? A dozen!
What he counted on was the truth. He did and said the truth,
and whether five, or five thousand, or five million responded
made little difference to him.

I should not say that it did not make *any* difference, because it did, but it did not change what he said or did. He
did not adapt himself to what the people wanted. Not that
he did not care about the masses, for he cared enormously;
but he knew that he could help the masses most not by doing
tricks, but only by being true.

We must now look at ourselves and the Church in the
light of all this that Jesus did, and we must try to do it as
honestly and frankly as we can, without exaggeration one
way or the other. It is fair, I think, to say that the Church
has not always followed its Lord in these less traveled ways.
It has on many occasions, but not always, and more especially, not the Church as we know it in the cities and suburbs
of the eastern seaboard of the U.S.A. More often it has taken
care to keep its own skirts clean rather than to get involved
with people whose reputations are shady, if not scarlet. The
Church as we know it, by and large, is a gathering of the con-
tented and the good; not the good, mind you, in the ultimate
sense, but the good in the sense of the law-abiding, the
custom-observing, and the socially acceptable. Among these
are many who are good in the deeper sense, but for the most
part the impression we make on the outsiders is that we are a
group of the well content, usually well off, and well meaning,
but completely cut off from the real facts of life.

And this we must recognize. The Church as it is today, no

matter what the figures may show, or what the statistics of the National Council seem to say, represents only a fragment of our society. I was conscious of it particularly when I was in New York. In a strange city, of course, you think of things that you do not often think of in your own home town where everything is familiar to you. But there when I saw the crowds on Madison Avenue, Lexington Avenue, First Avenue, Second Avenue, Third Avenue, I thought to myself, How many of these people are in any way included in the Christian fellowship? I do not know, but I had a feeling that not many of them were, and in the two churches in which I preached I saw no one who resembled them. The same thing would be true in Trinity Church, Boston.

The Church is only a fragment of our society, but it can be a powerful fragment. It does not have to be large to be significant, but it can be powerful only if it goes out to the others, in the sense that it is in communication with them. And this, let me say, and so clearly that no one may misunderstand, is not an easy thing to do.

In the first place, they are not likely to come to us. No matter how wide we open our doors, no matter how friendly and warm-hearted we are, they are not going to come to us, not many of them. Most of them do not want to live the way we want to live; many of them do not think the way we think, and have no desire to think the way we think; and many of them have no intention of living under anything like the discipline of Christ. They think we are either hypocrites or fools for even trying to do it. So they are not coming to us.

And it is extremely difficult for us to go to them. I hope I am not rationalizing. It is extremely difficult for us to go to them without either compromise or condescension, and I do not know which is worse. It is hard for us to go to them without seeming to compromise what we believe and what we try to do, or without seeming to come into their world as purists, condescendingly, patronizingly, to lift them up out of the gutter. It is difficult to be with them without either participating in their way of life or without seeming to patronize them. If you think that it isn't, try and do it.

In every city that I know of there are hundreds of people who spend the evening in bars, not because they are alcoholics but because they are lonely. Many of them are lost without even knowing it. My heart often aches for them, and yet I ask myself, how can I, or any other representative of Christ, go to those people without participating in what they are doing, or seeming to be completely patronizing and condescending? The only answer, of course, is to be like Jesus himself, so sure inwardly, so steady outwardly, that there is no doubt about your intention, and so vast in your compassion that there is no limit to which you will not go. It is difficult for us to be with people who are purely worldly in their way of living (and, if I may speak personally, I am with such people often, people who are materialists through and through) and neither condone what they do by seeming to enjoy yourself, which you do while you are with them, or condemn them for doing it.

Let me say that one of the clearest intimations of the divine depths that were in Christ Jesus was the fact that he could do both. He could be with people who were doing things that he knew were wrong without condoning what they did, or condemning them for doing it. He never compromised, he never condescended; he never condemned, never condoned.

That is God in human life. That is the understanding love of the Almighty in a human being.

Let him now speak to you. If you are one of the so-called "outsiders," remember that when the Prince of Men walked the ways of the world, no one was beneath him, no one. No one was beyond his care and interest, no matter what he had done, no matter how many times he had failed, no matter how bad a record he had. No one was beneath him. And remember also that there are people living now in whom his Spirit is alive. There are a few in every church; in some, many. They will never look down on you because they know that Christ never looked down on them. In his perfection, they have discovered their own imperfection and are prepared to meet you on the common ground of human frailty.

If you are on the inside, that is, if you are one of the members of the Body of Christ, if you belong to the Church and participate in all its activities, remember that when the Prince of Peace was alive in Palestine the people like you were the ones he could do the least for. Those who are in the Church are the ones that he can often do the least for because so many of them do not know that they need anything. They do not see where their shortcomings lie; they are protected by the superficial defenses and securities of life so that they do not really see the shallowness of their own existence. They do not realize that they have grown in years and yet cannot manage their inner life, control their temper, tame their passion, keep their mind on some far-off goal, no matter how their own fortunes may be rising or falling. They need someone who can help them, but they do not always know it.

Remember that as a member of the Church you are always in danger of becoming one of their number.

Also remember that when Jesus was on earth, no one was beneath him, and that if you are ever tempted to think that anyone is beneath you, the chances are that he is far above you. If you are tempted to treat a person as someone beneath you, remember how he treated those who were actually miles beneath him.

One of your chief assignments in life as a Christian is to be with people whom you may feel are beneath you in the sense that to date they have more losses than gains stacked against them. Remember that you are all in the same boat, if I may use that popular expression, that you are all sinners standing in the need of God, and that in his comprehensive sight the differences among you are slight.

Now read again the passage as it stands in the ninth chapter of St. Matthew's Gospel, "And it came to pass, as Jesus sat at meat in the house, behold, many publicans and sinners came and sat down with him and his disciples. And when the Pharisees saw it, they said unto his disciples, Why eateth your Master with publicans and sinners? But when Jesus heard that, he said unto them, They that be whole need not a physician, but they that are sick. But go ye and learn what that meaneth, I will have mercy, and not sacrifice: for I am not come to call the righteous, but sinners to repentence."

Go and do thou likewise!

HE *broke the law*

ON SATURDAY MORNING Jesus was in the synagogue. Among those present on this particular Saturday was a man with a withered hand. The Law said that a man could do no work on the Sabbath. God created the world in six days and rested on the seventh; all men therefore must rest on the seventh day of the week in honor of him. Healing a man could be interpreted as work, and therefore by some was forbidden on the Sabbath day.

Healing was as natural to Jesus as breathing, and "the guardians of the faith" were watching to see what he would do on this occasion. They were predisposed against him and were looking for an opportunity to discredit him in the eyes of the people. The atmosphere was electric. Would he heal the man, even though he had to break the Sabbath Law to do it? While they silently watched him, he looked at the man and said, "Come here." Then he looked straight at the men in the congregation, and it is almost impossible for us to imagine how penetrating a look that must have been. He put this question to them, "Is it right to do good, or to do harm on the Sabbath?" There was a dead silence in the synagogue.

You can see why. There was only one possible answer, and no one had the courage to give it.

Then the record goes on to say, rather surprisingly if you have not read it before, that Jesus looked around in *anger* at the faces of the men, *grieved* at the hardness of their hearts. One might stop right there and meditate upon the strange yet inevitable commingling of grief and anger in the character of the Master, and how these two go together in the lives of those who try to follow in his way.

Then he said to the man, "Stretch out your hand," and the man, who had probably not lifted his hand for years, stretched it out. He, like thousands of others then and now, could do what Jesus asked him to do. As he stretched out his misshapen hand, it was restored. Whether it was a case of psychopathic paralysis or some other physical malformation is not for us to inquire into at this time. The hand was for some reason crippled, and Jesus restored it to its original usefulness.

The story goes on to say that the Pharisees, the guardians of the faith, walked straight out and discussed with Herod's party how they could have Jesus put out of the way. The leaders of the religious institution turned to the leaders of a political party in the hope that their combined efforts might remove Jesus from the scene.

Let us first try to look at the situation from the Pharisees' point of view. I confess that I have never before tried to look at it sympathetically from their point of view. From the Pharisees' point of view, Jesus had broken the law. At least, he had broken the law as they understood it and interpreted it, and every lawyer will know what that means. He had broken not the law of the land, but the law of God. The law that he had broken did not represent the will of the people, as the laws on our statute books represent the will of the people of the United States. The law that he had broken, in the minds of the people, represented the will of God. God gave it to Moses, and Moses gave it to the people in ten monumental commandments, four having to do with man's relationship with God, and six with man's relationship with his fellow man.

These ten original laws had to be interpreted and applied to specific situations as they occurred. This is why there must always be lawyers, to interpret and apply a general law to a specific situation. For example, suppose a man wanted to visit a friend on the Sabbath. The friend lived five miles away and to get there he had to walk. It was a ten-mile walk, five miles each way, something more than a Sabbath stroll. Was it work, or not? The lawyers decided that the farthest a man could walk on the Sabbath day was two thousand cubits, a little less than a mile. Anything more than that was work. This man, therefore, was forbidden by the law to visit his friend.

These interpretations gradually formed a great body of law, all of which was considered by the Pharisees to be the law of God himself. To break the law was not so much a crime as a sin. This must be appreciated if the situation we are considering is to be understood. This is quite different from breaking the law in our system. In the eyes of these men, Jesus had broken the law and had therefore committed a sin.

Furthermore, this was not his first offense. He had broken this law before. One Sabbath day he and his disciples were walking through the grain fields. They were hungry, so they picked the wheat, separated the wheat from the husks, and ate it. The guardians of the faith said that they were breaking the law, for they were doing the work that a mill does when it grinds wheat. So this was not his first offense.

What is more, he had broken other laws. There were a great many ceremonial laws that had to do with the cleansing of vessels and the washing of hands before meals, and on more than one occasion Jesus had gone into a friend's house and eaten a meal without washing his hands. When he was brought to task for this he said, "It isn't the outside of the cup that needs to be cleaned, so much as it is the inside."

Great principles came out of these situations, and as Jesus moved through the difficult and delicate tension between the law and the lawyers, he left us the principle that the Sabbath was made for man, not man for the Sabbath, that the Law was a means to an end, not an end in itself.

He had broken this law, he had broken other laws, and he had even presumed to reinterpret the Law himself. He said, "You have heard, An eye for an eye, and a tooth for a tooth; but I say to you, If a man slaps you on the right cheek, turn the other one to him also."

My question to you is, What do you think you would have done if you had been in the place of the Pharisees? Here is a young man breaking a law which you believe to be the law of God. He is not only breaking it, he is presuming to rewrite it, and claiming for what he is doing the divine sanction. What would you have done?

I regret to say that some of you might not have done anything because you live in a day when respect for the law is at about the lowest ebb that it can reach. You might have said, if you had been in their place, "Well, of course, he broke the law, but everybody does it and there's nothing you can do about it."

On the other hand, you might have been one of those who realized that without law, without respect for it, without enforcement of it, we are not free to move about our streets, to live the kind of life we want to live as a community. You might have known that unless we live under law, we live in chaos. You might have known that you cannot write poetry except under law, that you cannot play a game without rules, that you cannot raise a family without rules and regulations, and that you certainly cannot build a nation without law.

If you are such a person, and if you had been in their place, it is entirely conceivable that you might have joined them as they went out of the synagogue, sincerely believing that for the good of the whole community and for the good of the social structure as a whole, this brash young innovator must be put out of the way. Any one of us might have been in that place.

Now let us try to look at the whole situation through the eyes of Jesus. The record does not tell us this, but if we use our imagination as we read, we can tell in an instant that the first thing he saw as he went into the synagogue was the man with the withered hand, a handicapped person, someone with part of his physical equipment paralyzed and useless. He was a man in need, and the immediate response of Jesus was always to relieve the need.

According to his understanding of it, the Sabbath law was intended to honor God. How could God, the Father of all men, be any more highly honored than by the restoring of one of his children to normal life? It is right to do good on the Sabbath day! Human need takes priority over parliamentary procedure, and the well-being of a man takes precedence over the rules and regulations of religious practice.

We must make it clear that Jesus did not always put the needs of people first, not always. When he was in the wilderness after his baptism, he was tempted to use the power he had to turn stones into bread to feed people who were hungry. He refused to do it. He said, "Man shall not live by bread alone, but by every word that proceedeth out of the mouth of God," that is, by every law by which the universe operates. So we cannot conclude from this story that human need always takes precedence over the law.

For example, if you are a student and you need to pass one course to get your degree, and the only way you can pass is to cheat on the examination, your need does not justify the cheating. Or, if you are a man in desperate need of a job, with a family to feed, and the only way you can get a job is to lie about another person who already has it, your need does not justify that lie. There are things which take precedence over human needs. But in this particular case, the need of the person took precedence over the meticulous observance of the law. The thing which we all have to learn is when to break the rule in deference to the need of some human being.

Then Jesus saw the Pharisees. He could see two things about them right away. First, because he was so shrewd in his understanding of human beings, he could see that they were not concerned primarily about the law for the law's sake, but for their own sake. The law and all that it meant created a system which gave them a kind of prestige by which they lived and on which they fed, and which gave them real satisfaction, and they would have nothing to do with anybody who threatened to destroy that system. This is a perpetual danger for every institution that exists, especially the Church.

We are all now concerned in what we call the ecumenical movement, the almost spontaneous movement of the broken fragments of the body of Christ toward each other. As we move toward each other, we have our own traditions, our own laws and ways of doing things, which mean a great deal to us. In our particular branch of the Church it is the episcopacy. The temptation is to keep the system, not only because it is good in itself, or because it is good for the people who belong to the Church, but because the system gives us a certain security and satisfaction which we do not like to give up. I know that there are many men in the Church who will speak for the episcopacy and fight to the death for it because they believe in it unqualifiedly; but I know that there will always be the temptation, in one form or another, to cling to it because it is precious to us and familiar to us; not because it is inherently good in itself, or because it is essential for the good of the people, but because it gives us a kind of satisfaction that we crave.

That is one thing he could see about the Pharisees. The other thing was that they were so preoccupied with the law that they did not even see the man with the withered hand. The law had become an end in itself, instead of a means to an end. Do you know how dangerous this can be in the Church? I can speak only of my own Church because it is the only Church I know, but in the Church we love, we have a certain amount of ceremony and ritual which we have inherited from the long distant past. The danger is always that the ceremony and ritual become an end in them-

selves, rather than a means to an end, the end being that
people may see more clearly the glory of God. There are
some people who are more concerned with what a minister
wears in the service and the movements he makes than they
are with the kind of person he is and what happens to the
congregation as he ministers to it. When ceremony becomes
a substitute for character, the Pharisees are alive again.

Looking beyond the man and beyond the Pharisees, Jesus
saw two things about people anywhere and everywhere who
make rules and regulations their religion. He saw that they
are likely to be proud of themselves. They are likely to say,
not in so many words, of course, but in effect, "Look at me.
I've kept all the rules. I've fasted twice in the week; I've
given a tenth of all that I possess; I've gone to church every
Sunday; I've received the sacraments on all the appointed
days. Look at me!" The terrible thing is that they are likely
to look down on other people whose record is not so good
as theirs.

Let me put this in your mind. Occasionally there is one
sentence which is more important than the others, one that
I like to drop in your mind in the hope that it will stay there
and grow. This is one of them. *Self-righteousness is a good
man's most dangerous pitfall.* There is nothing worse than
a man who thinks that he is better than anyone else.

He also saw that the same people are likely to think that
they are better than they really are, and you can see why.
The fact that they are correct outwardly blinds them to the
fact that they may be corrupt inwardly. This is the heart of
the matter. A man may not steal another man's possessions,
but he may steal his time, his attention, his energy, and in
the end possess him entirely. A man may not ever kill another

man, but he may go about with thoughts that are destructive, filled with bitterness and resentment, wishing that he could obliterate this one and that one; outwardly he is meticulously correct, but inwardly he is hopelessly corrupt.

We are trying to see more clearly what Jesus did in order that we may partake more fully of his life. We began with the extraordinary things he did, the miracles. Then we went on to the fact that he forgave sin, that he associated with outsiders. Now we come up against this rather unpleasant fact. He broke the law in the eyes of the best people of his day in order to fulfill a higher law, with the result that the law, both civil and religious, on Good Friday, broke him.

V

HE *prayed*

"WHEN JESUS HAD SENT the multitudes away, he went up into a mountain apart to pray; and when the evening was come, he was there alone." One of the things we know about Jesus beyond the shadow of a doubt is that he prayed. When the heavens opened at his baptism, and that one clear call of God came to him, what was he doing? He was praying. The night before he chose the twelve men who were to be most intimately associated with him in his incomparable task, what was he doing? He spent the whole night in prayer. After a strenuous day of healing and working with the crowds and the multitudes that were pressing in upon him from every side, what did he do? He withdrew himself into the wilderness and prayed.

Before he asked the disciples the question, Who do people think I am? — the crucial question that was to be the watershed of religious history — what was he doing? He was praying. When he was transfigured on the mountaintop, when the fashion of his countenance was altered and his raiment became white and glistering, what was he doing? The account in the Gospel says, "While he was praying the whole appearance of his face changed." The night before he died, where was he? In a garden, praying. When the end came and he was nailed to a tree, what was he doing? Praying, first for his executioners and then for himself.

The unmistakable impression that the Gospel leaves is that Jesus and prayer are inseparable. Think of the life of Jesus as a fine tapestry. If you try to pull out the golden threads of prayer, the whole fabric falls apart.

We now stop to make two observations about Jesus and prayer before we move on to the more urgent question about our own lives and our own prayers.

First, in most cases we do not know what he prayed about. How we wish we did! We know that on one occasion when his disciples returned from their first mission and reported to him their great success, he lifted up his eyes and thanked God for what had happened through them. We know that once he prayed that Peter would not lose his faith, but would keep steady. We know that once he asked to be spared from death, "Father, if it be possible, let this cup pass from me." And we know that once he asked God to forgive his executioners, and that he commended his own spirit to the Father.

But what took place during those long nights when Jesus was alone on the mountaintop we do not know, and I, for one, am thankful that there was still a place for privacy in those days. There was no one trying to pry into his private life and to take down in shorthand what he was saying to God. Thank heaven for that! I also would not wish to intrude upon it. I confess my curiosity, but I think it is not a worthy curiosity, and I am perfectly satisfied to think of him during those long nights in perfect unison with his Father. What passed between them I do not know, you will never know, no one will ever know, we do not need to know.

The second observation may be slightly less obvious. He never spent much time, as far as we can see from the Gospels, urging people to pray. It is a strange thing when you come to think of it, isn't it? He rather assumed that they did pray. Being human, knowing that they were dependent upon powers completely outside themselves, he assumed that they did pray in one way or another, and he proceeded to deepen and enlarge what they were already doing.

He assumed, for instance, that they prayed for their friends. He told them to pray also for them that despitefully used them. Do you see how he began to stretch the area of their prayer? He assumed that they prayed, as he did, in public, in the synagogue. He knew also that some of them prayed for display purposes, and he told them to go into their own room and close the door, and pray to God privately and secretly. "Pray in secret," he said, "and your Father who seeth in secret will reward you openly." He assumed, and quite right he was in assuming it, that they, like us, asked for things they wanted and needed, the necessities of life. He encouraged them to ask, but he went on to tell them, "Your Father knoweth that you have need of all these things before you ask." Ask, but be brief in asking. And the implication is, go on to other things, greater things, beyond your own little needs. Asking for things is only the beginning of prayer, the first step in an enterprise that includes petition the way parenthood includes requests.

It is interesting to notice that the only time in the Gospels that he tried to teach his followers to pray was at their own request. They went to him and said, Lord, all the other religious teachers teach their disciples how to pray and you have never taught us. Teach us to pray. Then he proceeded to do it.

This was so characteristic of him. So far as I can see he never told people to believe in God. He assumed that being human they did believe, in some way or other, primitively perhaps, inadequately perhaps, but he assumed that they did believe in God, and he drew the curtain aside so that they could see the full splendor of the Father's love.

He never told them in so many words that they were sinners. He never hammered away at their vices the way so many of his followers have been tempted to do. He began to open their eyes to the meaning of things, to what goodness really meant, to what keeping the law really meant, outwardly and inwardly as well, to what human relationships really ought to be, and what a man's relationship with God ought to be. And once they began to see these things, some of them at least began to see that they were sinners. Peter saw it like a flash of lightning when nothing at all had been said about sin.

Just so, he never told them that they must pray. He assumed that they did. Then, taking them from the shallows of their own needs and their own childlike prayers, he led them out, as it were, into the great deeps and said, When you pray say, Our Father, who art in heaven, hallowed be thy name. Thy kingdom come. Give us this day the bread we need. Forgive us our sins, as we forgive those who sin against us. And lead us not into temptation.

Out of the shallows into the deeps; all the nonessentials were stripped away, and the majesty of God and his kingdom, the necessities of men, their sins and their need for forgiveness, this was all that was left, all that was needed.

When we say that Jesus never told people to pray, that he assumed that they did pray, we are led to the inevitable conclusion that prayer was much more natural to the climate of his day than it is to the climate of our day. I doubt if any religious leader today would assume that, by and large, everybody he was talking to prayed as a part of his regular life. I do not think he would, for the climate today is quite different from what it was then. Sometimes it surprises me how quickly the climate has changed. It has changed radically within a hundred years, this spiritual climate in which men either pray or do not pray.

On July 1, 1851, a junior in Williams College, who later became a distinguished professor and a father of so many distinguished sons that he was almost like Abraham, wrote quite naturally in his diary, "As Henry and I were at prayer this evening, George Moar rapped at the door." That surprised me when I read it; two normal, healthy college students praying together as a normal part of the day's activity. I went on, and the diary revealed that what George Moar had come for was to tell the two young men whom he found at prayer that they had been accepted in a very worthy Greek fraternity, and that he and two men from Yale were there to initiate them on the spot. The son who has passed on to us the diary in a memoir of his father writes, "An invitation from this amiable brotherhood has frequently taken men off their feet, but I venture to question whether on any occasion since July 1, 1851, it has taken men off their knees."

I think he is probably right. He is right at least in the implication that people do not pray the way they used to. Some, of course, have never been brought up to pray. They have never been in families in which prayer was a natural activity. They are awkward when it comes to the act of prayer. Even a young theologian whom I admire greatly, and whose books I have enthusiastically recommended, when he begins to speak about prayer says, "I am deeply aware of my inability to say enough about it from the inside." Imagine a Christian theologian a hundred years ago saying, I hesitate to speak about prayer because I cannot say enough about it from the inside! And he goes on to speak rather timidly and shyly and with great winsomeness about "covering his own ineptness in prayer."

Some, of course, do not pray because they do not think it will do any good. They don't pray for the weather any more because they know that the weather is governed by laws which are not at all responsive to their personal requests. They don't pray for sick people because they believe that disease follows its own natural course, like a storm, and that neither the disease nor the storm will be deflected from that course by the request of a human being. They don't even pray for themselves because they have been taught to believe that they are what they are, shaped by inheritance and environment and all the rest of the equipment that they have been given, and that there is nothing they can do about it, or that anyone else can do about it.

What it amounts to is that they do not have anyone to pray to. The God who can hear the prayers of a human being and respond, that God for a great many more people in this country than we like to think, has been lost "in a crowd of stars." (I shall not quote the Yeats poem that those words come from, but you will remember a poem in which a rejected lover went out and lost his head among a crowd of stars.) I feel sometimes as though the God that people pray to has been lost among a crowd of stars in vast outer spaces; he does not hear and therefore cannot respond. In fact, there is no "he" at all. There are only things in general, and these have no mind and therefore cannot take notice of our cries.

I believe that most of us would grant that the climate has changed. People do not pray, even people in church, the way they used to. But also, I think we would agree that in the change we have lost something. This may reflect simply my own personal prejudice and point of view, but there seems to me to be a richness gone out of our air. There seems a depth gone out of our community life. There seems a confidence lacking in our personal life.

The same man who quoted from his father's journal when he was a student at Williams goes on to tell how when his father became a professor of economics, even though not a minister, he went every Sunday to preach in the church in South Williamstown. Listen to this very revealing sentence: "At many a four corners among syringa bushes rested a plain white house of God; and men of brains, men like my father, used to commune there with these people upon the deep things of life." His father communed not only with these people, but they and he together communed with the living God. We have lost this, largely; not entirely, but largely.

We turn, therefore, wistfully to Jesus. If you are drawn at all to him, he will draw you into prayer. If you are not drawn at all, of course, he will not, but if you are drawn to him, he will draw you into prayer just as he once did, and in the same way, not by telling you that you must do it, but by doing it himself. You will begin to say to yourself, as I have said to myself so many times when I have struggled with my own doubts, he knew too much to be deceived. He may not have known all the laws that govern outer space; he may not have known how the universe operates scientifically, but he knew things more important than these things, and he knew too much to be deceived. I cannot imagine that in those long nights when he was alone with his Father he was utterly deceived. I cannot believe it. Anything that occupied as much of his time as prayer did must have something more than some of us see in it, and cannot be beneath the consideration of any person, no matter how much he knows or how highly educated he may be.

Also, he never tells us exactly what prayer is, never once in the Gospels. He begins now as he did then with what we have. It may be only a cry in the night. Then he starts to train and deepen that primitive cry. I knew a portrait painter who was engaged to paint a portrait of a person that he had not seen for eighteen years. He thought he knew the person, but during the eighteen years the person had changed, and when the sitter went for the first sitting, the painter looked at him and said, "I've got to get a bigger canvas." It wasn't that he couldn't get the person on the canvas he had prepared; it was that there were moral and spiritual proportions in the person that a canvas of the original size could not possibly suggest.

I keep hearing Jesus say to me, You have got to get a bigger canvas for your prayer. It must be larger than your little needs, important as they are; it must be large enough to include more than your cries in the night. It must be a canvas great enough for the grandeur of God and his will and his purpose, and until you get that larger canvas, prayer will mean nothing to you. If you persist in thinking of a God sitting above the heavens, ready to pull strings here and there to make things come out right for you and for those you love, your prayer will gradually wither away.

And finally, he will almost surely lead us away from the crowd into some quiet place. He slipped away into the wilderness. He went up onto the mountain apart, alone, to pray. In some ways there is nothing like public prayer as it takes place in a House set aside for that purpose. But it is no substitute for solitude. You will never find what Jesus meant by prayer until you are alone with God.

Then you say to yourself, Where in the world can I find such a place? If you are young, you say, My house is in a constant turmoil with children, and dishes, and a thousand chores that have to be done. And the city has its noises, and confusion, and dirt, and distraction. Where can I find such a place? I can tell you. A church, any church.

I have never been one to desire to begin movements, but if there is one movement I should like to start this is it. I should like to begin a movement in which the members would promise, when possible, to spend twenty minutes a day in a church, some church, somewhere. At first they might not know what to do. They could just sit still and let the currents of God sweep over them until they begin to feel them, and the time would come when they would know what to say. You say twenty minutes is too long, nobody can afford that amount of time. Ten minutes is too little. It is better than nothing, but you cannot get really unwound in ten minutes. You have to sit still long enough to do it. To drop on your knees and say a prayer and dash out is better than nothing, but it is not what Jesus meant by prayer.

The same theologian who confessed his ineptness in prayer writes later on: "All we know is that somehow our style of life must make room in our world of noise and movement for the silence, the waiting, the withdrawal of the life of prayer." * How well we know that! Knowing that, we look to Jesus and we say, Lord Jesus, take us apart from the world; teach us to pray; show us the Father.

* William Hamilton, *The New Essence of Christianity*, Association Press, 1961.

Note: Some of the material in this chapter appeared in the Introduction to *Book of Prayer for Everyman*, published by The Seabury Press, and is used here with their permission.

VI

HE *went to Jerusalem*

ON PALM SUNDAY Jesus rode into the city of Jerusalem on a donkey just at the time when crowds of people were pouring into the city for the celebration of the Passover. His appearance caused quite a stir in the city, especially among the pilgrims. People along the way suddenly began to cheer. Some, in their enthusiasm, even took off their outer garments and spread them in his way. Others cut branches off the trees and waved them as they shouted and cheered, hailing him as the King of the Jews, the Son of David who came in the name of the Lord. It was, indeed, a spontaneous acclamation of Jesus by the people.

I think it safe to say that there were no religious leaders taking part in the demonstration, no theologians, no priests, scribes, or Pharisees. Sometimes the plain people are quicker to recognize the truth than the professionals, particularly when religion is involved. I can say this because while I am not a professional theologian, I am engaged in a religious profession, and I know from the inside the truth of what I am saying. Theologians and trained experts in religion can often get so wrapped up in their theories that they miss what a plain man sees instantly, and as clearly as he sees the light.

For a few brief moments the entrance of Jesus into Jerusalem looked like a royal procession. We do not know whether this was the specific intention of Jesus or not, whether he deliberately planned so dramatic an arrival or not. There is no way of knowing. All we know is that when he entered Jerusalem, he entered it riding on a donkey, and that an anonymous prophet had once said that when the ideal king came, he would come in just this way, as a man of peace riding on an ass, "the most universally useful domesticated animal in Palestine." We also know that for those few great moments there were crowds of people who treated him like a king; and we know that the Christian Church ever since has understood his entrance into Jerusalem as a declaration by him of his right to rule in the lives of human beings. That much we know.

Most of the people in the city had no idea what it was all about. They didn't even know who he was. They did not have the means of communication that we have. When John Glenn rode up Broadway, everyone in New York knew who he was because they had seen him on television, heard about him on the radio, and read about him in newspapers. But most of the people in Jerusalem had never seen or heard of Jesus. They did not have the faintest idea who he was and when they felt the stir that he created, they asked, "Who is this?" The answer they were given was, "This is Jesus, the prophet, from Nazareth in Galilee."

One wonders how you could tell the truth more accurately without coming anywhere near the truth itself. True, Jesus was from Nazareth, and Nazareth was in Galilee; no one could contradict that. True, Jesus was a superb teacher, and in that sense a prophet; no one could contradict that. And yet, to say that and nothing more about him was about as far from the truth as you could conceivably be. Suppose a stranger visited this planet of ours and landed in the United States of America, and asked someone, Who is this Abraham Lincoln that I hear the Americans talking about? Suppose then that the answer to his question was, He was a rail-splitter from Kentucky. That is an absolutely accurate statement of truth. No one could possibly contradict it. He was a rail-splitter, and he came from Kentucky. And yet, how far this undeniably true statement of fact is from the truth about the Great Emancipator!

Who is this who so strangely, yet persistently pursues us through the centuries? Who is this Man to whom we are drawn, even though we do not do what he says? Who is this? "The image of the invisible God," writes one man in the New Testament. "The Word of God made flesh," writes another. "God of God, Light of Light, Very God of Very God," proclaims one of the creeds. What do you say? What is your answer, for in a very real sense every man has to answer this question for himself. He may be guided by others, he may begin with the experience he inherits from those who have gone before him, but he will never have a real answer to this question until it is his own.

Thirty-two years ago it is that Nathaniel Micklem, one of the English theologians, principal of one of the Oxford colleges, wrote a book called *Mysterium Christi*, and I go back to it from time to time. It comes from the generation of my theological school days and it still speaks to my condition. In it there is this sentence: "For today, as ever,

Jesus is called divine, not primarily because of Church traditions of His life and teaching, but because of what, as Redeemer, He has done and does for the souls of men."

Your answer to the question will depend largely on what he has done for you. If he has never stirred you, as it is entirely conceivable (and I know many good people who are in this group), if he has never made you feel uncomfortable as though you were in the presence of the Most High God, if he has never rested you with the peace of God which passeth all human understanding, and lifted you up above the confusion and discord of life into a higher realm; if he has never done anything like this to you, never made you feel forgiven, never made you long to forgive others because you yourself have been accepted, then no matter how faithfully you repeat the answers of other people, they will mean little or nothing to you, even though they be the meticulously correct answers of the most orthodox believers.

When I was in college I took a course in Shakespeare. It was given by a man who at the time was the most famous Shakespearean scholar in the world. I learned a great deal about a few of the plays. I learned as I had never known before how words change their meaning, and I learned a little at least of what English words meant when Elizabeth I was Queen of England. I memorized hundreds of lines, long since forgotten, and I learned what the best minds thought about Shakespeare. I was in a responsive mood and was receptive to everything I heard. I did not question it; I accepted it all.

Several years later I made a friend who lived and breathed Shakespeare. He both produced *Hamlet* and played the lead-

ing role himself in one of our eastern universities. It was the
first time a student drama group had ever done such a thing.
You could not be with him for long without meeting Shakespeare and, since he lived in the room directly under mine,
I saw a great deal of him and consequently met the Bard of
Avon often. He never analyzed the plays, he never tried to
explain the words to me, but one night, quite late, he came
into my room unexpectedly, and said to me, "Would you
like to hear a scene from *Hamlet?*" And without the book,
he began the Third Act, and went on and on, taking all
the parts himself, in a voice that was unforgettably beautiful.
Then I knew who Shakespeare was.

It is very much like that, only on an infinitely greater
scale, with Jesus. You are interested in him; you are born
into a Christian tradition; you study the things that other
people have written about him; you learn the creeds; you
read the New Testament. All this is of infinite value. You
are responsive to them, you accept them all in the sense that
you do not reject them. Then sometime you may be reading
the Gospel all by yourself, and in a flash you will meet him.
Or, you will meet a person and he will say to you, not in the
same way that my friend said it about Shakespeare but in a
different way, Would you like to hear the story of Jesus?
And he will tell it to you, not in terms of history, or theology,
or creeds, or intellectual theory, but in terms of his own
life, and you will begin to feel what Jesus has done in the life
of that man. You will get the impression that he is alive
in him, and through him he will touch you. Then you will
know who he is, the Ground of your existence, the Goal of
your hopes, the Love of God focused upon the fragile,
transient life that you are trying so seriously to live.

To get back to what happened on Palm Sunday, you remember I am sure, how it ended. The spontaneous acclamation faded away with the setting sun, and denunciation rose to take its place. We must not be too harsh on the people for what they did. This is not to say that what they did was right; it is only to understand it. It is not very difficult to see why they did what they did if you look carefully and think clearly, for Jesus, our Lord, asked the people to do something that even though they wanted to do it, and some of them surely did, when it came to the point of actually doing it, they couldn't.

To put it in a few words, what Jesus asked them to do was to be servants instead of lords. He asked them in their whole attitude toward the whole of life to be servants instead of lords. Think what that meant! It meant *taking* orders instead of *giving* them. It meant putting themselves *under* authority instead of exercising authority *over* people. It meant being willing to take the lowest place instead of fighting for the highest. It meant suffering instead of fighting. It meant stripping life of its luxuries and getting down to its essential simplicity. It meant trusting God instead of relying on themselves. It means walking the earth quietly and reverently, not strutting like a peacock.

They couldn't do it. They couldn't do it any more than we as a people can do it. Individuals attempt it, and some come very close to it. But can you imagine this nation today saying, We surrender all our claims to power wherever it is exerted in the world. We lay aside all our armaments, and we begin this day to serve the people in the world wherever there is any need to be served. Can you imagine the nation saying that? Practically speaking, it is impossible.

Ultimately speaking, nothing else is possible. There lies the human dilemma; there is the situation from which men longed to be saved.

The question comes to my mind, and I wonder whether it ever does to yours, If this is so, why in the world do we go on celebrating Palm Sunday year after year? If the whole point of it is that our present way of striving, grasping, fighting, ruling by force or threat of force is wrong, and we have no intention, or at least no prospect or expectation of changing it, then why do we go through this every year? Are we not being utterly hypocritical?

I think not. We do it because what we do not do, what we know we ought to do and wish we could do but cannot do, he did! He laid aside every claim to power, he stripped himself of all the things that mean power in the world, in order that he might do the will of God. And in some strange way, that is so mysterious that we can never explain it, what he did we somehow share, and as long as we remember what he did on Palm Sunday, we know that we are not entirely lost. What he did somehow takes the curse off our failure, and as we identify ourselves with him we are lifted up onto higher ground.

We do it because there is something in us that rises to his way. When George VI, the late King of England, died there was a short article in a magazine which described his unusual reign. He came to the throne, never expecting to sit upon it, and he did it under the most difficult circumstances of world war, with a graciousness that was almost unbelievable and that warmed the hearts of the English people. The article concludes with this line, "Perhaps his reign has helped us to realize that graciousness is an attribute of true power, and that humility is closely akin to majesty."

Infinitely more so, what Jesus did makes us realize that power without humility is weakness, and that humility is closely akin to majesty, that there is nothing great in the world ever achieved apart from it. No man ever wrote great music or great drama or great poetry, built a great building or led a great movement, who did not put himself aside and say, What happens to me is of no importance: I am here to do the will of him that sent me.

So we rehearse year after year what Jesus did on Palm Sunday, and so long as we keep before us what he did on that day, there is always the possibility that from time to time, in our imperfect way, we will do it too.

Let no man deceive you. You will do it too. Drawn to him into a new way of life, catching if only for a few minutes, perhaps, his Spirit, you will have the grace to say, Not unto me, Lord, not unto me, but unto thy name be the glory. Not my will, but thine be done.

VII

HE *died*

ON ONE FRIDAY in the spring of the year we stop to remember something that happened almost two thousand years
ago. That in itself is extraordinary. In a world where so
many things are happening and where they are so quickly
forgotten, it is extraordinary that any single event should
make such an impact upon the consciousness of men that it
has the power to draw them almost two thousand years after
it happened.

It is even more extraordinary when you remember what it
was that happened. A young man was put to death on the
double charge of blasphemy and treason. He was completely
unknown outside his own country and rejected by most of
the people inside it. The country was no larger than the
state of Vermont, a minor province in a huge empire.

But just as among the thousands of books that are published year after year there are one or two which rise
above the others because of some unmistakable greatness, so
there are a few human events which rise above the sea of
lesser things that are happening all the time. They are the
high moments in human history when the mute is taken
away and the strings of the spirit soar to incredible heights;

60

when men are at their best, and are sometimes better than you could ever believe them to be; and when things happen that bring God close to men.

It is no wonder that we human beings like to relive these high moments. We like to remember them because a great deal of our life is monotonous, often sordid, with little or no relief from its steady drone. From time to time we like to relive the high moments of the exaltation of the human spirit and to share, even though vicariously, in their splendor. It is interesting that most of these moments occur in the hour of death. The death of Socrates is one of them; the death of Jeanne d'Arc is another. In our own country the event that we most often remember when we are thinking of its human greatness is the death of Abraham Lincoln. And the two plays in recent years that have most deeply moved their audiences have to do with the death of a man. One has to do with the death of Thomas à Becket; the other with the death of Sir Thomas More.

The particular event which we are now remembering likewise has to do with death, the death of Jesus. You remember it, at least vaguely. You remember the outline of the story, but you want to remember it vividly, in detail. You want, if it is possible, to relive it. This we shall try to do by concentrating our attention on the traditional seven last words from the cross and on the situation to which they were addressed.

I cannot vouch for the literal accuracy of the words, or for their chronological order. There were no reporters present. Only one is recorded in St. Matthew's Gospel, and the same one is in St. Mark's. St. Luke adds three others not recorded in either St. Matthew or St. Mark, and omits the one which they include. St. John adds three other words which are not mentioned in any other account. These facts do not suggest the literal accuracy of the last words of Jesus.

But there is a higher accuracy than the accuracy of the letter, and that is the accuracy of the spirit, and of this I have no doubt. Whether or not Jesus said these words exactly as we have them, and in the traditional order, is to my mind relatively unimportant. What is important is that they speak to us, that they ring true to everything else that we know about Jesus, and that they tell us something about God, about life, about death, and about ourselves; and above all, they tell us what Jesus did when he died.

As we relive this event, we will realize that it is not something that we are simply observing dispassionately the way we might study the accounts of the Battle of Waterloo. It is not like that at all. It is something we are taking part in. In a very real sense the shame of it is our shame, the guilt of it is our guilt, the glory of it is our glory, and the power of it is our power.

And we shall see, perhaps for the first time, that this event is not one of the high moments in human history, one among many others, but the highest one of all, and in what I shall say about it I shall assume that there is something eternal about it, something that reaches beyond the years, and that as we try to relive it we shall be reaching into eternity where the years are gathered together, fulfilled, and finally lost.

Let me state plainly the object at which we are aiming: our object is to relive the death of Christ that the life of Christ may be relived in us. Our purpose is not only to remember that storm which one writer describes as a storm

which shook the world, but also to be shaken by that storm
out of our complacency, our blindness, our doubt and despair, into a new life of trust and hope and love.

This will not happen to everyone who reads these pages
because not everyone is ready to receive it. There are some
people who are not yet ready to hear about this mighty event.
They will put the book down before the end not only because they have something else to do which seems to them
to be more important, but because it does not speak to their
condition.

I am told that there are people who see the Grand Canyon
for the first time and turn away unmoved. If that be true,
how much more likely is it that there will be some who see
what Jesus did on the cross and turn away unchanged.

But those who have ears to hear and eyes to see may be
drawn into something deeper than they have known before.
There is nothing in the story that they have not already
heard, but hearing it again, at this particular moment in
their life story, they may go more deeply into the meaning
of it. They will explore the unsearchable riches of Christ's
life and death, and great things may be added unto them.

i

We notice immediately that one of the first things that
happened on the cross was that Jesus prayed for the people
who put him there. He asked God to forgive them on the
ground of their ignorance. "Father, forgive them; for they
know not what they do." In his compassionate eyes, they
were like children tearing to shreds a precious Rembrandt

with no idea of the value of what they were destroying.

We know that all the deviltry in the world is not by any means the result of ignorance, and that there are people who set out to do evil and who know exactly what they are doing. But we also know that there is a great deal of evil in the world that is the result of ignorance. I wish I knew how many children hurt their parents without the slightest idea that they are hurting them, and how many parents hurt their children without the faintest notion that they are hurting them, and without any intention of doing it.

Presumably, in this prayer Jesus included the soldiers who did the actual work of execution. We are told that there were four of them. Also included in the prayer were the officials, both Roman and Jewish, who were really responsible for what the soldiers did. (It is futile to try to place the blame on one or the other. A good case can be made for the original guilt of either the Jews or the Romans, but looking at the scene from this distance, we can see that both Romans and Jews had their part in it.) He also included in his prayer the people who stood by and did nothing, or who ran away and refused to accept any responsibility for it.

The amazing thing is that he was able to see and think about the people who were taking away his life completely apart from himself. When someone is hurting you, not superficially but deeply, can you treat him objectively, with no reference whatever to yourself? Occasionally you can. If you are a parent, you probably can. Or, if you are a husband or wife who adores his mate, you can — sometimes, but not always. You almost always think of people in reference to yourself and what they are doing to you. But here

is Someone who could and did think of people who were
hurting him completely apart from himself. He was so absorbed in what he was doing that what people did or said
about him made little difference to him. He had reached
that stage of maturity, which to my mind is the ultimate
stage, in which he had shed the protective self-consciousness
that is sometimes so blinding and crippling; and he had shed
it by losing himself in the Kingdom of God. Or, to put it
more accurately, because he was completely absorbed in
what he was doing, what people did to him was of only
incidental significance.

One thing I know is that there is no other way of shedding
that protective covering. Some people, I suppose, have it
more than others, but the only way you can get rid of
your defensive self-consciousness is to lose yourself in something great. Only as you lose yourself in something far
greater than yourself, something that demands all that you
have, are you free from yourself; free from your vanity,
which everyone has to some degree; free from your fear,
which everyone has in one way or another. Only then are
you free to forgive, to overlook, to understand, to treat
people as they are quite apart from anything that they are
doing to you.

Not long ago I read a story about an actor whose name I
do not remember. He told how he began. He was given a
part in a play in which George Arliss, one of the most distinguished actors on the English-speaking stage of his day,
played a leading role, and in which he had a relatively minor
part. This, however, was his great opportunity. The morning after the opening night when the reviews appeared in
the newspapers, there was a rather unfavorable and un-

pleasant reference to George Arliss, and a glowing account
of the unknown actor. At the next performance George
Arliss called him to his dressing room, to dress him down,
he feared. When he entered the room, Mr. Arliss said, "My
son, I want to congratulate you!" George Arliss was so
absorbed in the theater, so secure in it, that he could look
at this young actor completely apart from himself, without
a trace of jealousy, or without anything that might have
poisoned his relationship with him.

This takes practice. Anything that is worth much does.
As far as I can see, we are not born with a character. We
have to grow one. We have to shape it as we go along. One
of my elderly friends told me years ago — she happens to be
a lady, and a perfect example of what she said — "If you
want to be a gracious old lady at seventy, you must begin at
seventeen." If you want to be a forgiving, understanding
person at seventy you must begin at seven.

We are mistaken if we think that because Jesus was God
incarnate he achieved this freedom from self without practice. He began when he was a boy to be about his Father's
business. It absorbed him more and more, and the more it
absorbed him the freer he became, and the less concerned he
was with himself and his own future. So by the time he came
to die, in his early thirties, every drop of bitterness had been
drained from his soul. Even if we were talking about him
only as a human being, this puts him in a class by himself. I
wonder if there is a single person reading this book who
has not one drop of bitterness toward anyone. Perhaps there
is; I hope so. I often think that I do not have any, and
then just as I think it, I begin to taste the gall.

This, then, is what Jesus did on the cross — he forgave all those who had any part in putting him there. What good did it do, you say? None, at the time. No one changed his course. Pilate was deeply impressed but not converted. Caiaphus, the high priest, was not even impressed. The soldiers did not fall on their knees in penitence. The crowd did not rally around him. Flights of angels did not come to his rescue.

Goodness so often seems to be like that. You make a real effort to do something good, it may be something heroically good, and what comes of it? Nothing. No one seems to notice it. In fact, many times you get into more trouble than you would if you had not done it.

Remember two things. Real goodness is never done for the sake of anything but itself. Jesus did what he did for one reason only; it was the right thing to do. It was the will of God. Whether anybody paid any attention to it, whether it ever "paid off" in converts or in consequences of any other kind, was beside the point. It was the will of the Father who sent him. That is the first thing to remember.

The other is that goodness always bears fruit, but in its own way and in its own time. The first performance of Bach's St. Matthew Passion was on April 15, 1729. At a recent performance an annotator wrote, "Unnoticed when first performed, unknown elsewhere, until Mendelssohn brought it to light a century later in Berlin, thereby starting a general awakening to the greatness of Bach."

It was less than a century after the death of Jesus that Stephen brought to light what Jesus had done on the cross by dying in the same spirit, with practically the same prayer on his lips, "Lord, lay not this sin to their charge," and thereby started a general awakening to the greatness of the love of God in Christ.

And since then, how many people have felt the forgiveness of God because of what Jesus did on the cross? Obviously, we cannot produce any statistics, but how many people do you suppose during the succeeding centuries have felt the forgiveness of God because of what Jesus did? And how many people have forgiven others because of what he did when he died?

Only a short time ago a minister of a Protestant church in a neighboring town accidentally struck and killed the wife of a policeman. The policeman and his wife were Roman Catholics. Theirs was one of those blessed marriages of unbroken happiness, but when friends went to see him after the accident, he said, "I have no animosity toward anyone. I am only sorry for the man who did it." Whether the spirit of that man came directly from what Jesus did on the cross, I cannot say, but I am sure that it is part of the climate that was created on that Friday in the spring of the year so long ago.

What happened on the cross was that Jesus brought to a focus the forgiving love of God upon the foolish ways of men, so that men who had been forgiven would themselves be moved to forgive others.

Think now of any grudges or grievances that you have against anyone and as you think of them, let them go. Knowing that you yourself are forgiven, you can now forgive those who have trespassed against you.

ii

The next thing that happened on the cross was that Jesus was drawn into a brief conversation with the other two men who were being crucified at the same time. They were both criminals, commonly referred to as "thieves" or "robbers." What the nature of their crime was we do not know, but it is hard to imagine a more vivid demonstration of the unfair distribution of life's rewards and punishments. Two men who had made a failure of life, and between them the Prince of Men, all three subjected to the same torture.

The sooner we learn that what happens to us is not always what we deserve, the better prepared we will be to meet it. Sometimes when we make a mess of things we pay for it, and pay for it dearly right away, or very soon. But sometimes we do not, at least not for a long time, and often it seems to us as though other people who make a mess of things go scot-free.

On the other hand, there are times when we outdo ourselves in goodness, at least according to our own evaluation, and we enter at once into the joy of it; but there are other times when we suffer more than the ones who have behaved badly. The sooner we learn, I repeat, that what happens to us is not always what we deserve, the better we will be able to handle the things that do happen to us. Remember that there were once three men, two were acknowledged thieves, one was the Son of God, but all three died by execution, all three came to the same humiliating end.

Looking at the two men on either side of Jesus we see

that they both had more or less the same history; both were
failures. We pause a moment to remember how many failures
there are in life, how many buds that never bloom. Also,
neither one had any previous knowledge of Jesus, at least
not so far as we know. In the account given by St. Matthew
and St. Mark they both joined in the sneers and jeers of the
crowd saying, If you are the Son of God, why don't you
come down from the cross? But St. Luke picked up a story
— we do not know where, perhaps from one of the women
— according to which the two men were quite different
in their response to Jesus.

One, to be sure, railed against him, If you are the Christ,
why don't you get us out of this? But the other rallied to
his defense, How do you dare say such a thing? Leaving aside
for the moment the question of historical accuracy, this is
true to life, is it not? People exposed to the same opportunities
often respond in completely different ways to the same thing.
Many times there is no way to account for it. Two people
brought up in the Western world and educated in more or
less the same tradition can see at the same time Michel-
angelo's David in Florence, and one will say, Big, isn't it?
and the other cannot say anything at all because he is too
moved to speak. Two different responses to the same thing.

The same is true of our response to Jesus. Two children
are brought up in the same Christian home, exposed to the
same Christian teaching. When they confront Jesus one of
them says, So what? and the other says, My Lord, and my
God! So we are prepared for this difference in response
which rings so true to life.

Out of the blue, the thief who rallied to the defense of
Jesus asked him to remember him when he came into his

Kingdom. "Lord, remember me when thou comest into thy Kingdom." What do you think he meant? What do you think he really wanted? We have no way of knowing, with any certainty, exactly what he meant, and the more you read the commentaries, the more puzzled you are likely to be. The better way is to search your own inner longings, the things you want and need, the things you are asking for, and the things you dread, and in them you may see a reflection of what this man wanted.

For one thing he wanted recognition — "remember me." Perhaps he had never had any real recognition in his life. It is surprising how many people there are even in these enlightened days, when parents are trained in every conceivable branch of the art of bringing up children, how many children never have had any real recognition, any real appreciation. Perhaps this criminal had never had any real recognition; perhaps if he had had when he was young, he might not have been where he was on this particular Friday.

I wish I had kept a record of the young people who have come to me in trouble, not in scrapes with the law necessarily, but with their own desires and drives, and who sooner or later revealed the fact that at least in their opinion their father and mother never really paid much attention to them. They were well-fed children, starving for affection and recognition, and the lack of nourishment in their youth reaped its deathly harvest in their later years.

There is something in us that demands attention and craves recognition. I do not mean the sensational recognition of the spotlight, the compulsion of the prima donna to be always in the center of the stage. The desire for that sort of recognition many of us have but we try to weed it out as

we grow into maturity. The recognition which I am thinking of is the quiet appreciation of someone who really cares,
and really loves us. Without that kind of recognition no
human being can keep his head above water.

The thief wanted recognition particularly at this moment
because he knew that he was about to venture into the unknown, and when he made that venture he wanted to be
known by someone. I do not know how you feel about
death; I do not suppose any of us will ever really know how
anyone else feels about it. I have been with many people
who were near death, and I have gone through the valley
with a few, but I would not dare say how they felt about
it because they took their secret with them. I suspect, however, that it is not so much death that you dread as it is
the thought of being unidentified, not recognizable; the
way I, with my peculiar temperament, feel when I go into
a strange town where nobody knows me. I think to myself,
Oh, if only someone would come along and call me by
name. It would make the barest town beautiful.

The thief also wanted another chance. At least we have
the right to imply that he did, for we are putting ourselves
in his place, and we call him "the penitent thief." He knew
that his life had been a failure, that he had missed the opportunity that God had given him, that he had missed the
bus, so to speak; he wanted a chance to try again. And seeing
Jesus gave him the hope that there might be another chance.

There are times when we feel that we have not made as
much of our lives as we might have; at least I hope you feel
that way sometimes, because if you do not, it means that
your vision is dim and that your sights are low. I often feel
it at the end of a summer holiday abroad; when I come home,

no matter how much I have enjoyed it, I invariably think to myself, I did not make as much of it as I might have.

When we realize that we have not made as much of our lives as we might have, we almost inevitably ask, Will we have another chance? Sometimes we think, yes; and sometimes, no. I was pleased to read in a book called *Elegy of Manhattan* by George Jessel, the popular entertainer, this statement: "It is good and heartening to believe that the scenes we act in this world are not the end of the play." There are many times when we feel exactly like that, that the end of the earthly scene is not the end of the play. But then we read the words of Albert Camus, written in a more serious vein, and infinitely more shattering than the previous statement, "I do not want to believe that death opens out onto another life. For me it is a closed door." It is a closed door for a great many people. Often, too often, it is for us.

If that door was once closed to you and is now open, even though only on a crack, what opened it, or who opened it? What always pushes it ajar for me is an encounter with someone whose life is too great to be measured by purely earthly dimensions, someone too great to be written off, blotted out, or plowed back into the earth, someone who lives a life so abundant that the more death presses it down, the more it runs over. And when I see Jesus, when I hear him say, "Today shalt thou be with me in paradise," the door swings wide open.

I cannot define the words. No one knows exactly what "paradise" means in the New Testament, and it occurs only in this single instance. But it suggests pure and uninterrupted delight, the kind of bliss that you catch a glimpse of once in a great while but cannot detain for long. And you feel the immediacy of the words; you sense the personal concern of the One who said them. And as you hear them, you know that Jesus took the fear out of the future by putting himself into the present.

I know that there are many people who fear the future; some because they are old and they do not know what will happen to them in the twilight years; some because they are young and they fear that the world may blow up in a nuclear holocaust, or will peter out with a whine and a whimper. My prayer is that any fear of the future you may have will be taken away by letting Jesus be in the present. I cannot tell you how to do it in any specific words. I only know that when the Lord God in Christ is with us in the present, we can leave the future to take care of itself, and can live in the present freely, responsively, and joyfully. Even though we may be going through a dark valley, we know that he is with us, and where he is there is life.

iii

After Jesus had spoken to the man beside him and given him the assurance of the recognition which he longed for, he turned his attention to a completely different situation. It involved his mother and who was going to look out for her. There were, according to the Gospels (e.g. St. Mark 6:3) other children, four boys and at least two girls, all younger than he, and by this time undoubtedly married with families of their own. When Jesus died, Mary was left virtually alone, with perhaps twenty more years to live, and with the disabilities of old age, disease, and death ahead of her.

It is worth stopping at this point to remember how many are the companions of Mary, alone in the world with no one in sight to help them, no one to stand by them through the dimly lit years. There are more of them than you think.

Be that as it may, Jesus saw his mother standing there, and beside her one of his friends. He said to his mother, "Woman, behold thy son; son, behold thy mother." ("Woman" was not a severe but a respectful word to use in addressing one's mother.) In other words, he was asking his friend to look out for his mother, and his mother to accept the care and attention of his friend. "And from that hour that disciple took her unto his own home."

It is sometimes true that our friends are closer to us than our own family. It often comes to us with a bit of a shock when we suddenly realize that we are bound together not so much by the natural ties of blood as we are by the supernatural ties of the things we love together. So it was that this middle-aged woman, probably fifty, and this young man were bound together by the fact that they both loved the same person. And how many people in the world do you suppose have been bound together in the same way, and by the same person?

The first thing that comes to your mind as you think about what Jesus did for his mother is that he was not aloof to this very human and altogether common situation. It is surprising, in a way, that St. John is the only one who catches this particular glint from the cross. It is at first surprising because in St. John's Gospel Jesus is the glorified Christ from beginning to end. He is never tempted; he never prays for help, not even in Gethsemane; he knows what people are thinking before they speak; he has no hesitation at all about the cross; he never shrinks from death, and he goes to Jerusalem to carry it himself in triumph; he makes tremendous claims for himself, "I am the resurrection and the life," "I am the light of the world," "Before Abraham was, I am."

And yet, it is in this same Gospel that Jesus meets a woman at the well because he is sitting there resting, tired after a long walk; and when his friend dies, he weeps. And it is in this Gospel that Jesus stoops, as it were, from the cross to look out for his mother.

I think it is safe to say, though people do not agree about this, that Jesus in his adult years had not always been close to his family, not even to his mother. Someone once said that it is not easy to be the wife of a great man, and I am sure that it is not. If that be so, surely it must not have been easy to be the mother of the Son of God; to watch the child grow up into a man, and to see him choose paths that were hazardous and that would inevitably lead to destruction was not easy; and to hear him say things that were beyond the range of a mother's human understanding was hard.

But death drew them more closely together. How often it is so. We normally think of death as the great divider, the separator that tears asunder people who love each other deeply. Yet in another, more kindly aspect, death sometimes draws people together who have been apart for years, draws them into a union closer than they had ever known before.

The fact that Jesus was not aloof to this situation reminds us that the Christian Gospel is about a God who became man and who, becoming man, took upon himself the problems, pains and perplexities of man's existence. It is the story of one who stooped low, who drew near and went with them on the way; who healed their wounds, soothed their sorrows, and drove away their fears. It is the incomparable story of one who came to seek and to save those who were lost.

It reminds us that if and when the Christian Church is aloof from the human situation in which ordinary people find themselves, its day is done. When the Church ceases to care for the sick and the aged, when it ceases to be concerned about the alcoholic and the mentally disturbed, then it ceases to continue the ministry of Jesus in the world. When the Word which it preaches becomes so abstract and theoretical that it has nothing to do with the aches and pains, the anxieties and dilemmas which the people are facing, it will be a hollow word with only the echo of death for a sound.

When I spoke sometime ago about the possibility of building a nursing home, one person who is a faithful member of the Church said to me, What has the Church to do with that? Why should the Church take on an undertaking such as that? My answer was, If the Church ever comes to the point where it does not take on things like that, its days are numbered. To be sure, Jesus did not come to make men comfortable but to give them a new life; but he often did it by lifting some of the burdens of the life they already lived.

Another thing that immediately comes to mind when you hear these words is that Jesus met her need not only by giving her someone to look out for her, but by giving her someone to look out for. She needed both, and so do we. We need someone to look out for us when we are not able to look out for ourselves, and we need someone to look out for. One reason, I am convinced, why so many lives look like streams that have dried up before their time is that while they have people to look out for them, they have no one to look out for. Their outgoing energies are locked up within themselves and, not being in circulation, eventually dry up.

You may have read the story of Spencer Tracy's son, John. He was born deaf. His father discovered it one day when he spoke to him and realized that while he was old enough to hear, intelligent enough to respond, he paid not the slightest attention to what he said. The father's spirit wilted at the thought of a deaf child. When the boy was four years old, his mother, Louise Tracy, took him to Boston to see Dr. Harvey Cushing. In recalling the visit which was both the end and the beginning of her hopes, she described it in these words: "Dr. Cushing said, 'There is nothing I can do, Mrs. Tracy, but I just want you to know that you're blessed among women. In helping John, you can lead a wonderfully interesting life.' I've never forgotten those words."

In 1942 she founded the John Tracy Clinic at the University of Southern California. Her plan was to educate other parents of pre-school deaf children to win their battle as she had won hers. More than six thousand children have been helped to lead more normal lives. One person looking out for another, and in doing it, finding his own life. This is the secret. So many of us think that we find our lives when we are looking out for ourselves. We need someone else to look out for us when we are not able to look out for ourselves, but what we need most of all is someone whom we can look out for and into whose life we can pour our affection and intelligent care. That person may be standing near you now.

Remember Mary. Remember John. Remember how Jesus on the cross brought them together in a new relationship in which each looked out for the other, and in so doing, he saved them both. In Christianity we speak constantly of salvation. It means so much that sometimes it means nothing. For it to mean something real we need to see it grounded in some specific situation such as this. Here are two lives saved by the fact that they were linked together in a new relationship of mutual responsibility.

That may be too simple for some people, but it has been confirmed in my experience over and over again through the years. At the very time when everything seems to be slipping away and life itself hardly worth living, Someone steps into the picture and saves the situation, first by caring for me and then by teaching me to care, and by giving me something to do.

Some of us are facing loneliness, some of us are leading lives that are empty. We now ask God to bring us together so that each may find the other, and in finding each other we may find ourselves. And we ask him to spare us from ever thinking that the Christian Gospel is something too aloof to be concerned with things like these, how people are going to get along in their old age, how young people are going to be related to the older generation. These are things which God will help us work out together, and thereby save us from being completely surrounded by nothing but ourselves.

iv

At this point in the traditional story of what happened on the cross, Jesus had responded to every person on the scene. He had prayed for the soldiers and the spectators; he had listened to the two men on either side of him, and saved one from his dread of the future. He had provided for his mother by committing her to the care of his friend. When there was nothing more for him to do, he cried.

According to St. Matthew and St. Mark, he cried out with a loud voice, "My God, my God, why hast thou forsaken me?" The mystery of these words lies forever beyond the reach of our understanding, and every time I come to them I feel how unworthy I am, or anyone is, to say anything about them, for who dares plumb the depths of the divine mind? Whatever we say about them, therefore, we say in penitence and humility, acknowledging that what we say is only our imperfect, yet sincere attempt to draw more closely to the mind and heart of Christ.

As we think about these words, the first thought that comes to our minds is that it is not the existence of God that Jesus is questioning; he is not asking whether there is a God or not. It is the action of a God who does exist that he is questioning. My God, my God, why do you do what you do, or why don't you do something that you haven't done?

Humanly speaking, of course, it is altogether understandable, and it is at this very point that the cross reaches most deeply into our troubled lives. The first three words are a moving proclamation of the ministry of Jesus, but this word is a revelation of his own inner, secret self. As we watch him our own hearts are ready to break when we see that after Jesus had looked out for everyone else, it seemed to him that no one was looking out for him, not even God.

Beginning with ourselves, we know that there are times when complete darkness descends upon us, and that sometimes we have brought that darkness upon ourselves. A cashier in a bank has been slowly but surely swindling money from the bank through the years. Finally he is caught. He has a wife and family who know nothing about his criminal activity and who are the innocent victims of his crime. The bottom drops out of everything. In the darkness he cries, but as he cries he knows that he brought the darkness on himself.

Yet there are other times when we know that we have not brought it on ourselves, at least we cannot see that we have. We have done the best we know how with what we have, and yet we seem to be the victims of the worst that can happen. When that kind of darkness falls upon us, we cannot help but wonder why it should be so.

I remember reading in September 1960, when the crisis in the Congo was at its peak, an article by James Reston. In the first part of the article he pointed out that Khrushchev seemed to be the hero of the day. Then he went on to say, "The real hero of the day was the Secretary General of the United Nations. Mr. Dag had just proved an important point, namely, that intelligence and persistence applied to principle sometimes prevails over physical power." When I read that, I cheered. One year later, when the plane that was carrying Dag Hammerskjold to another trouble spot went down, I found myself virtually crying, crying out, What was God doing when that plane went down? Why did God let it go down? Why didn't God save this man who could do so much for the peace of the world?

True it is that God works in a mysterious way his wonders to perform, but there are times, are there not, when it seems that he is not working at all, that he has quit for the day, and left us to work things out as well as we can, to sink or swim. This is all the more bewildering when, after he has enticed men to give up everything for his principles, he seems to give them up to the mercy of physical power.

Whatever the reason for the darkness, we know that we would never suffer this particular kind of darkness, and the anguish of it, unless we loved the light. No human being, at least so far as I know, is immune to suffering of some kind, physical, moral, or spiritual, but not all human beings suffer in this particular way. It is a mark of maturity when you suffer this kind of pain, a sign of sensitivity that is uniquely human. You would not be deeply hurt when a noble person failed, or when a good cause was abandoned, unless you cared about something more than the safety and comfort of your own life. You would not be hurt by the absence of God, or by what seems like the absence of God, unless you had known the wonder of his presence.

It is the believers, the lovers of God, who are destined to this kind of suffering. I warn you of that now. You can avoid it if you want to by steering clear of the light and of him who is the Light of the world, and you will never know it when the light flickers and finally goes out. You will never miss it. But if you have ever known it in the full brightness of its glory, then when it begins to burn dim and sometimes seems to go out, you will suffer the tortures of the damned.

No President, I believe, who ever occupied the office was more completely controlled by belief in God than Abraham Lincoln. Yet listen to these words that he wrote early in his life when he was being criticized for not being a believer in the technical sense. "Probably it is to be my lot to go in a twilight, feeling and reasoning my way through life, as questioning, doubting Thomas did. But in my poor, maimed way, I bear with me as I go on, a seeking spirit for a faith that was with him of olden time, who in his need, as I in mine, exclaimed, 'Help thou mine unbelief.'" In other words, there is a darkness that only the most dedicated will ever know; there is a desolation that only the most sensitive will ever fully taste.

In the light of these things it seems almost inevitable to me that Jesus should go through this kind of darkness. If the faith of the most dedicated mortals is inevitably accompanied by hours of darkness and doubt, and it seems to be undeniably so, then it is not likely that Jesus, the most dedicated man who ever lived, was spared either the darkness or the doubt. If the more sensitive a man is to the Divine Presence, the more likely he is to be aware of what seems to be his absence, then it is not hard to believe that when everyone had deserted him, and the skies were dark and threatening, Jesus thought that God had deserted him too.

If you think of Jesus as God disguised as a man, then this will have no meaning for you. But if you think of him as a real man who in the very depths of his manhood disclosed the very nature of the Godhead, then this is inevita-

ble. If you think of him as a man whom God chose to be
his own channel and instrument of self-revelation, using
every single facet of his human nature to manifest some aspect
of his own love, then this experience of being separated
from God himself is inevitable, for this is an intrinsic part
of human existence from which not even the man Christ
Jesus could be spared.

I should like to lead you one step further. There is a
line in the Psalms which reads (it is one of those great lines
that ought to be accompanied with timpani and trumpets,
the instruments that in our refinement and delicacy we
seldom use in our worship of God), "The Lord is King,
the earth may be glad thereof." And then, following closely
upon that proud proclamation, there come the somber
words, "Clouds and darkness are round about him." It was
a real insight to recognize that there were clouds and
darkness as well as glory and light, that there was mystery
as well as meaning, sorrow as well as joy. But in the Psalm-
ist's vision the clouds and darkness were apart from God.
They were "round about him." He was in the midst of them,
but unscathed by them and in the end, master of them.

There is something in this vision that is ultimately valid
and true. And yet somehow when I come to this word from
the cross, it seems to me that it takes us even one step
further, for when I hear them, and when I see him who
said them, I say to myself, the clouds and darkness are not
apart from God; they are a part of God. He is in them and
they are in him. When, therefore, you and I go through
terrible experiences and feel as though we were separated
from God, we say to ourselves in our moments of clarity,
This is all part of God's way with us; the clouds and dark-

ness are not around him, they are in him. And what is more, he is in the clouds and darkness. For was there ever a time when God drew nearer the earth than at the moment when Jesus thought he had been forsaken?

This is one of the mysteries of life. We will search it but will never fully penetrate it. We can only remember that the clouds and darkness are not around him, they are in him, and that when the clouds and darkness surround us, we may be in him, and he may be in us. Say to yourself, The mysteries are so great, the power so incalculable, the love so broad, so deep, what then shall I fear?

V

The next thing that happened was that Jesus asked for a drink. "I thirst," he said. There was a bowl of sour wine there on the ground, and someone, probably one of the soldiers, took a sponge and soaked it in the wine and put it on the end of a spear and pushed it up to his mouth. It was the pain that made him ask for a drink.

Jesus, as far as we can tell from the Gospel narrative, had not had much physical pain to cope with in his life, not much compared to other people. He had never had the pain that often goes with extreme poverty. His people were working people, and lived the simple life of people who earn just enough to get along on. But he was not brought up in a slum, nor did he go through the kind of degradation that some children brought up in the slums of New York or Boston have to put up with. He never had the pain that comes with prolonged illness, nothing like

Paul's nervous disorder that he called "a thorn in the flesh." Apparently he was a strong, healthy young man, and for that we thank God. Not until the very end of his life did he have a real taste of pain.

Notice that even then he had done nothing to deserve it. Quite the reverse. He had spent most of his life trying to relieve the pain of other people. I shall not dwell upon this because I have already spoken about it. I shall pinpoint it for those who may have missed it, or for those who may not have taken it in. Pain is not parceled out on the basis of merit. Far from it. Those who are most deserving often suffer most, and those who are least deserving often suffer least.

While Jesus was relatively free from physical pain, he was never free from the much greater pain of the spirit — the pain of disappointment, misunderstanding and frustration. Of the two, this is by far the greater pain, and the agony of the spirit is more terrible than anything that the body can suffer.

When he finally did experience physical pain in these last hours of his life, he took almost no notice of it. I often wish that we could catch just a glimmer of this sublime indifference to our aches and pains. We spend so much time talking about them. Jesus barely mentioned his. He had more important things to talk about. We act as though suffering were something alien to us. I find this true of myself and also of many people with whom I deal rather intimately; we are inclined to resent any kind of physical pain as an interruption, an intrusion upon our serenity, a violation of our happiness, the way I am likely to resent bad weather on a holiday, as though the whole season were planned for my pleasure.

C. S. Lewis says in a preface to one of his books, "We should stop expecting so much. We are not going to know ultimately; we are not going to enjoy every last minute of life." Think about that for a minute. "We are not going to enjoy every last minute of life." He goes on to say, "Our expectations of the world and life are often simply fantastic."

And we waste a great deal of time trying to figure out why such and such a painful thing should happen to us. People often ask me, Why should this happen to me? I say, Why shouldn't it? There is nothing special about you. (I confess to you that I am not quite so quick to say it when it happens to me, but I try to.) This is part of our human experience. Who are we that we should be spared what the very greatest have had to bear?

From time to time I like to call the roll of the great who have suffered most. From year to year I add new names to the list. You already know them, but once in a while it is valuable to remember them, and to recall that their achievements came out of great tribulation. I have recently added the name of Vincent Van Gogh because his paintings are being exhibited once again at our museums. He suffered the worst of all pain, the pain of mental torture. Read his letters if you want to know more about it. John Milton was blind; Beethoven, deaf; Pasteur, partially paralyzed at forty-six, his speech paralyzed at sixty-five; Pascal, that most sensitive spirit of the seventeenth century, mathematician and genius in the realm of the spirit, never had a day without pain after his eighteenth year; Charles Darwin for forty years never knew one day of health as ordinary men know it; Robert Louis Stevenson was a chronic invalid; Thomas Huxley had long periods of depression; Thomas Carlyle, the grand old craggy Scotsman, described his body as "that rotten carcass every avenue of which is changed into an inlet of pain"; Immanuel Kant, who did more to change the thinking of the Western world in the last hundred years than any other single person, writes, "For a long time I have been accustomed to regard myself with a degree of health so small that many would have complained." Our beloved Abraham Lincoln wrote in 1841, twenty years before he became President, "I am now the most miserable man living. If what I feel were equally distributed to the whole human family there would be not one cheerful face on the earth." I now add one other name because he suffers a kind of pain that I know something about. Pablo Casals, the veteran cellist, one of the greatest musical minds alive, writes, "Nerves and stage fright before playing have never left me throughout the whole of my career."

What shall we then say to these things? If pain seems to accompany these tremendous creative accomplishments, shall we seek it for its own sake? God forbid! Shall we cease to relieve it in others, and in ourselves, when we can? Of course not! But when it comes we will accept it as a legitimate part of life. Carl Jung, in an article on happiness which appeared in an English newspaper several summers ago, wrote that even a happy life cannot be without a measure of darkness, and that the word "happy" would even lose its meaning if it were not balanced by sadness.

Pleasure and pain go together like everlasting twins. And

you can remember, if this is any consolation to you — I am
not sure whether it will be to everyone — that creation
and pain almost always go together, from the mother who
bears the child, to the man who brings forth some great
work. No pain, no great thing done. We might almost set
it down as one of the laws of life that the higher we climb
on the ladder of spiritual maturity the greater will be our
exposure to suffering and pain.

This, then, we can do; we can accept the suffering that
cannot be relieved. But we can do more. The cross always
leads us on to further ranges. Just as when I come back
from a holiday I always feel that I have not made as much
of it as I might have, so I feel in a strange way that the
cross evades me, that I have never quite reached it. You
think you are there, but you are never quite there. You
think you know what the cross says about pain, and at that
very moment it begins to point to something more.

We can do more, therefore, about pain than accept it
as a legitimate part of life and remember that creation and
pain go together. We can expect something from it. Do
you think you can ever learn to expect something from
pain and suffering? A friend of mine, not long ago, turned
me once again to Edith Hamilton's *The Greek Way*. In
it is a quotation from Aeschylus, who lived almost five
hundred years before Jesus. Read it carefully. "God —
whose law it is that he who learns must suffer. And even
in our sleep pain that cannot forget, falls drop by drop
upon the heart, and in our own despite, against our will,
comes wisdom to us by the awful grace of God."

It is one thing to read that in Aeschylus, to recognize

academically that there is truth in it. It is another thing
to see it on the cross, and to take it to yourself, as you
take up your cross and follow him.

vi

When the end was near, Jesus said, according to St.
John, "It is finished." If you did not know the context you
would not have any idea what the words meant. They might
be simply a statement of fact, a serene recognition that
everything that has a beginning must sooner or later come
to an end, every day, every book, every storm, every holiday, every life. So, Jesus might have been saying, Like every
other life, my life now comes to an end. This is the end
of my time, less than average in length, more obscure than
some in fame and success. But be that as it may, one thing
is certain, it is finished. The curtain has been rung down
and the drama is ended.

Or, they might be a sigh of relief. It is finished; thank
God it is over. No more arguments with the legalists, no
more disappointments from those who might have understood but did not, no more long stretches in the wilderness
where the bouts with Satan recurred again and again, no
more long nights sweating it out alone on the hillside, no
more narrow escapes getting out of town just by the skin
of my teeth, no more struggles to try to make them understand, no more putting up with stupid people who have
no imagination. It is finished; it is over.

Knowing the context, however, you know that they
could not possibly mean either of these things. The words

are in St. John's Gospel, and St. John's Gospel is the story
of how God revealed his glory in the life of Jesus Christ.
The glory is never hidden from beginning to end. Not a
single shadow ever crosses it. When Jesus feeds five thousand people, it is the glorious Bread of Life that he gives
them, which if a man eat he will never again be hungry.
When Jesus raises Lazarus from the dead, it is the glory
of the resurrection and the life. When he heals the man
born blind, it is the glory of the light of the world which
nothing can put out.

So when he says, "It is finished," he can mean only one
thing. The revelation is complete. There is nothing more
to be said or done. You have seen the glory of the eternal,
and if you do not see it, nothing more can be done to make
you see it. You have seen the perfect obedience of man to
God, and the perfect love of God to man, these two in one
communion and fellowship, in one single life. There is no
more to see. It is done, gloriously done.

To be sure, life moves on. New situations will develop;
new discoveries will be made, new achievements, new
flashes of light here and there, and we must keep our eyes
and ears open, heaven only knows, to all these things that
are going on round about us. But in a sense these confirm
what has already been done. They neither change nor add
to the revelation.

This is hard for some people to take in. Perhaps an experience of my own will help to make it plain, although
it is miles and miles from what I am trying to say about
what Jesus did when he died.

When I was in college I happened to be in Bethlehem,
Pennsylvania, at the time when the Bach B Minor Mass was

given, and I went. I had never heard it before. I did not
know very much about it, but as I heard it, I said to myself, This is music. And when it ended I thought, There
is nothing more to be heard. I have heard a great deal of
music since then, great music, different music, contemporary music as well as classical, but in that music was the
revelation of what music really is, and all other music
either measures up to it or falls short of it.

A great many people have that experience when they see
and feel what happened on the cross. They say to themselves something like this: This is the love of God; there is
nothing more, there is no more to be said or done. This is
the revelation of the glory of God, and the glory is the
glory of love, suffering, forgiving, serving, offering itself
completely, utterly; this is the glory. You cannot go any
further. No matter what else may happen, it will either
fall short of it or measure up to this Love. It cannot go
beyond it.

The revelation has been made. The response is yet to
be made, and the wonderful thing is that when the response
is made by people like us, imperfect though it be, the revelation reoccurs. The light, the love, the life that was in him
is seen again.

It is finished, and it is never finished. The revelation appears before our very eyes; we make the response; and the
reconciliation takes place. For this we thank God.

vii

According to St. Luke, Jesus prayed just before he died.
According to St. Mark and St. Matthew, he cried out in

agony, and according to St. John, he made a simple statement of fact. But as St. Luke remembered it, he prayed.

It is not surprising that the writers of the Gospels remembered and reported different things. No two people reading this book will see and remember exactly the same things. What they see and take in will depend a great deal upon what they want to see, what they are ready to see, and what they need to see. So it is now; so was it then.

We must be careful not to judge too severely those who see or hear things in the cross that we cannot see and hear, and not to be too harsh with people who do not see or hear what we see and hear.

At the very end of his life, St. Luke heard Jesus praying, "Father, into thy hands I commend my spirit." It is doubtless a prayer that he had said all his life, from early childhood until now. But it is not a child's prayer and the implications of it are vast. It implies that behind all the bewildering events that are shaking the world, in the very heart of the mystery that so often baffles us, and in spite of the evil that at times takes hold of us and is always a threat to our existence, there is someone we can call Father, someone who knows what it is all about, someone we can trust with our life, someone who knows us, who loves us, and who gives himself for us.

Jesus believed that; there is no question about it. He was brought up in a family that believed it. He lived in a world which in general believed it; not everyone of course, but on the whole people believed it and lived their lives accordingly. He died believing it, in spite of all that had happened to him during his brief earthly course. People do not often change in their basic pattern. They grow, they

develop, and they alter as they grow, but the pattern that
is there at twenty you can usually find if they live to be
ninety. The original theme remains; the variations upon it
are sometimes endless. Jesus began trusting God as his
Father and he died doing exactly the same thing, the only
difference being that the trust at the end had been tried,
tested and matured, strengthened and developed.

The question for us is, Can we believe it? Can we believe
anything comparable to it? Our world is very different from
his world and consequently we are different from him. We
know much more than he did about the world we live in,
about the sea around us and the sky above us. We know, for
example, according to a report made not long ago by a
group of astronomers, that there are twenty galaxies, clouds
of stars and hydrogen gas just like our own galaxy, whirling
in space at an average distance of ten million light years
from the earth, and that the twenty are a sampling of one
million or more "island universes" strung out through ob-
servable space. In a universe like that, can we still say, "Father, into thy hands I commend my spirit"? A great many
people cannot and do not; they feel that in their understanding of the universe they have outgrown the simple
trust of humanity's childhood.

Questions like this are too vast for any one person, let
alone myself, to presume to answer. But I venture to suggest one or two things which may point to the answer.

For one thing, size, by itself, is beside the point. If it took
the creative mind of a man to make the first automobile,
how much more will it take the mind of a man to manage
the modern plant which produces hundreds of automobiles
each day? If you cannot have one flower, or one child, or

one star, without the creative imagination of a mind that conceives it, how much less can you have a million or ten million without such a mind? The presence of one flower, one child, or one star, is no less mysterious than the presence of a billion. The vast size of the universe makes it more difficult for us to picture the Father who loves and cares, while at the same time it makes it more urgent upon us to try.

When I wonder how I can believe in the God who is the Father of us all, as I do at times because I live in the climate of this present world and, because I am a minister, I am not immune to the currents that other people are affected by, I remember with satisfaction the uneducated mother of a son who, after he had been graduated from college, went home with his diploma and his proudly won knowledge to tell his mother what it was all about. She looked at him with love and understanding and said, "You may know more than I do, but I know better."

You see, I hope, how to apply that to the cross. Our Lord, as the image of the invisible God, says to us from time to time, You may know more about things in the universe than I do, but I know better than you about the things above, beneath, within, and beyond the universe; I know better than you about the things that you can really trust and build your life upon and to which you can give your loyalty. You can count the stars; I will count my loyal friends. You can shoot for the moon; I will shoot for the human heart. You can trust your own ingenuity; I will trust my Father.

An editorial appeared in the *New York Times* shortly after John Glenn had made his three phenomenal orbits around the earth in outer space. The writer made this striking statement: "We are not helpless in the great depths of space any more than John Glenn was. We may be guided by some destiny whose nature we can scarcely comprehend, just as Colonel Glenn's capsule was guided from the ground." When I read it I immediately paraphrased it in words something like these: Just as Jesus was guided through the valley of the shadow of death by some destiny that we may not completely comprehend but that he called Father, so we are not helpless in the depths of space.

How is it that in this world, so torn by trouble and suffering, sin and disease, we get the lasting sense of so much love? For me it is from one perfect Life no shadow ever crossed, when man's obedience and God's love met together in one communion and fellowship.

So Jesus died. The conclusions which men have drawn about the meaning of his death are too numerous even to mention. Beginning with St. Paul, men who have felt the full impact of his death have been bound to reinterpret the whole of existence in the light of it.

In this book I have only hinted at some of the conclusions which men have drawn from the death of Christ, and have concentrated as intensely as possible on the event itself, hoping that you may draw a conclusion of your own as the result of your participation in the deed.

To give you a clue to what I mean I remind you that Anglican chaplains in the First World War were severely criticized for their ineffectiveness. But there were outstanding exceptions. One was T. B. Hardy, a schoolmaster parson, who at the age of fifty insisted that he go to the front as a chaplain. His heroism was incredible. He refused every offer of safety and was finally killed. In describing his death, William Purcell in his biography of Woodbine Willie writes, "In Hardy so many of the failures of others seem somehow redeemed and forgiven."

This, on a small scale, is the clue to what we feel, on an infinitely larger scale, when we witness the death of Christ. In and by his death, we say, the failures of others are somehow redeemed and forgiven.

VIII

HE *rose from the dead*

ON EASTER our chief concern is not to speculate about the possibility of our own survival after death, nor to discuss the immortality of our own souls, vitally interesting as that may be. Our first desire is to celebrate the resurrection of Jesus Christ from the dead, and my purpose in this chapter is to tell you something about his resurrection in such a way as to make you feel it as you may not have felt it before, so that you can celebrate it with all your heart and soul and mind.

This is not an easy thing to do. For one thing, the resurrection of Jesus is an event entirely unrelated to anything else that you know anything about. There is nothing like it in your own experience, nothing to compare it with, nothing to relate it to.

In the last chapter we looked long and intently at the cross, and the cross has to do with sin, suffering, and death. You know something about all three. You have sinned. Even though you may not call it that, you have felt the twinge of conscience, you have done things you know were wrong. You have had your share of suffering; perhaps you have had more than your share. You know what pain is; you know what it is to suffer a broken heart. And you have been in the presence of death; though you yourself have not yet been through it, you have seen others go through it; you have felt the chill of it.

Easter, on the other hand, has to do with something completely outside the range of your experience. You have never known anyone who has died and come back to life. I am not thinking now of those rare instances in which a person's heart stops beating for a few minutes, and then begins to beat again. That sort of phenomenon, wonderful as it may be, is in no way comparable to what happened on Easter. On Easter a man who was dead and buried came to life again.

The fact that there is nothing like it within the range of your experience is one reason why it is so much more difficult to speak about the resurrection of Jesus than it is to speak about his crucifixion.

Added to that is the fact that the climate in which we live is more favorable to the tragedy of Good Friday than it is to the triumph of Easter. The present condition of the world breeds pessimism, starves optimism. Think of the playwrights, the poets, the novelists, and the artists you know. More often than not their theme is the meaninglessness of existence, and it is a pessimistic note that prevails in most of their work. They are more at home in the vicinity of the cross than they are at the empty tomb, and they are more eloquent when they speak of evil than when they speak of good.

Also, the scientific atmosphere in which we live encourages the layman to think that nothing is real unless he can either see it or use it. The scientists themselves do not think this, mind you, but we lay people have gradually come to think it as a result of the enormous emphasis that science places on experimentation and observation. Unless we can see something, measure it, handle it, and use it, we think that it has no value at all. In fact, if we cannot see it or hear it, we assume that it does not exist. And this same scientific atmosphere that we all have grown up in makes us suspicious of anything that cannot be put down in black and white, labeled, named, catalogued, analyzed, and doubly suspicious of anything that appears to break one of nature's precious laws. You can easily see that the resurrection of Christ does not flourish in a climate that is favorable to things that are tangible and visible.

One thing is certain, whatever we say about this strange and unprecedented event must be in some way related to our personal experience. At least it must be so in my case. There are people who say in utter sincerity, I am sure, that you accept the resurrection of Christ on faith, meaning that you take it into your life as a sort of foreign body, without seeing what it means, without imagining how it could be, with reference to anything else in your life, and without any experience of anything else even remotely related to it. I cannot do that. I am not made that way, and it would mean nothing to me if I pretended to do it.

I can accept what the scientists say about the atom on that kind of faith, and I am willing to do it, but it makes not the slightest difference one way or the other in my life. I cannot do that with the resurrection. Granted that I do not pretend to understand it, that I see it always sheathed, as it were, in mystery, I still cannot accept it without reference to the rest of my experience. When I speak, therefore, about the resurrection of Christ, I must do it in reference to my own experience, knowing that it is limited, partial, and imperfect, and in the hope that I can relate it to yours.

Where shall we begin? I begin with people, the people that I know, the people who are living now. I have seen people come to life who were virtually dead. I do not mean physically dead, of course. I mean people who are morally as limp as a rag, spiritually without any motive or incentive at all. When you look at them, they look like a deserted house, with all the doors and windows boarded up, and not a light to be seen anywhere, not even through the cracks. I have seen people like that come to life.

I have seen others who might well be dead and buried under the burdens that they carry, burdens of responsibility and suffering, and what looks to me like unendurable pain. These people, I say, who might well be dead and buried are borne aloft as though on invisible wings by a life greater than theirs. I have seen this.

What is the secret? They have all had a transfusion, not of blood, but of life, and the life is the Life of Christ. They may not call it that, they may not think it is that. They may not know what it is, but the interesting thing to me is that the identification marks are always the same, and are unmistakable; the outstretched arms, the outgoing love, the all-embracing understanding, and the complete absence of self-concern; the print of the nails in their hands, the signs of suffering and sacrifice, the scars of pain; the trust that is written all over their faces and that wipes away every trace of strain and anxiety, and underneath all the cuts and bruises, all the shocks and jolts of life, the joy that no man can take away from them, but which everyone catches from them.

I say to myself, No dead Christ could do that to anyone! A wire that lights an electric bulb is a "live" wire, and
a Christ who can bring a person back to life is a living
Christ. I begin with this, with what I see happening in people right before my eyes.

Then I go back and read the Gospels. I am not implying
that I had not read them before, and I know that if I had
not, I should not have interpreted what I saw in the people
the way I did. I know that. But I still say that I begin with
the people, and then go back and read the Gospels.

I read the resurrection stories over again. I read how the
women went to the tomb on the first day of the week as it
began to dawn, and found it empty; how Peter and John
ran to the sepulchre, and how John got there first but,
because of some strange inhibition in his personality, he
did not dare to go in, so Peter went in first; how two men
were walking along a country road and a Stranger came up
from behind and went with them on the way, and stayed
for supper; how the friends were huddled together in a
little room with every door closed, and suddenly Christ was
in the midst of them.

I see the discrepancies in the stories; I see the contradictions; and I see quite clearly that they do not all match
perfectly. I am intelligent enough, I think, to be aware of
the manifold difficulties, and sufficiently unprejudiced to
admit that they are there. But it seems to me more and more
as I grow older that the picture is blurred by the very
brightness of it, and I, for one, would not have it otherwise.

I, personally, cannot agree with the one who says that
we may believe in the living Christ only if we believe in
his "corporeal resurrection." "Corporeal" in English means

bodily, or material. In the Gospel stories I see the risen Christ appearing in different places at the same time, passing in and out of closed doors, and finally rising into the heavens out of sight. This is not what I should call a "corporeal" presence. But it is a Presence, nevertheless, so real that in the effort to describe it, men used corporeal terms.

Without that Presence there would be no New Testament at all, no Sermon on the Mount, no parables, no story of the cross. These were remembered and finally written down because they were told by, or about, the one who had risen from the dead. Without that Presence you would not be reading this book, because the Christian movement would have died a natural death a few weeks after the crucifixion.

Exactly what happened on the first Easter, I do not know, and I am bold enough to say that I do not think anyone else does. I confess that I am always a little suspicious of people who think they do, and more than a little impatient with those who are dogmatic about what they think they know. But I do know that over him who offered himself in perfect obedience to the will of God, death had no dominion; sin had no claim whatever upon him, evil never got the best of him, suffering never soured him, and in the end, death could not possibly hold him. I know that he is alive the way electricity is alive, the way energy and spirit are alive.

Finally, I turn to my own personal experience, limited as it is. It is not exactly the same as yours, but I hope that we have enough in common as human beings, and as Christians, so that as I speak of my experience, it will ring a bell in yours and bring to the surface things that may have been buried. I know, for instance, that when I am concerned about myself, all wrapped up in myself, thinking only about myself, what I am going to do, how I am going to appear, I die. I know that when I love, when I forget myself, when I lose myself, I live. I know that. I know that I rise when I forget myself.

I know that when I am helpless and feel that the things I have to do I cannot do, there is Someone greater than I who helps me. In ways I cannot predict and sometimes do not recognize the help comes. I know what St. Paul meant when he wrote, "I can do all things through him who strengtheneth me."

I know that time cannot take away the things that are most precious to me. I know that in some strange way God is the beginning and the end of all things, and that in the midst of this mysterious life which involves so much suffering as well as joy, there is the One who came and lived among us, died for us, and now lives in us.

I think I know what Richard Wilbur, a poet teaching in Wesleyan University, meant when he wrote about the milkweed, the common milkweed that you have seen in New England dooryards.*

> *Anonymous as cherubs*
> *Over the crib of God,*
> *White seeds are floating*
> *Out of my burst pod.*
> *What power had I*
> *Before I learned to yield?*
> *Shatter me, great wind:*
> *I shall possess the field.*

* From *Advice to a Prophet and Other Poems* by Richard Wilbur (Harcourt, Brace & World, Inc.).

From time to time I know from personal experience that when I yield, when I am apparently shattered, I possess the field. But to see the full magnitude of this truth I must look beyond myself, beyond all my heroes, to my Lord and Master. Jesus yielded. Jesus was shattered. Jesus possesses the field.

"Christ is risen from the dead, and become the firstfruits of them that slept. For since by man came death, by man came also the resurrection of the dead." Thanks be to God!

IX

What He *did then is relevant now*

THE UNITED STATES RESUMED the testing of nuclear weapons over Christmas Island in the South Pacific on Wednesday in Easter week of 1962. I mention this not to introduce, as you might expect, a discussion of the question of nuclear testing. This is a question, highly complicated, about which Christians will have to think more seriously than they have in the past, and about which they will not always agree. I mention it, rather, to raise an even greater question suggested by the place, and especially the time of the testing. I wonder if any of you were struck by the fact that it was over *Christmas* Island that the bomb was dropped, on Wednesday in *Easter* week.

The question that this raises in my mind is, does the victory of Christ over death have any real relevance to the world in which we really live? Suppose that on an Easter Day you were a stranger from another planet, and you went into a Christian church. You would feel the note of triumph and victory, you would hear the people sing:

> *The strife is o'er, the battle done,*
> *The victory of life is won;*
> *The song of triumph has begun. Alleluia!*

Then suppose that you began to look around the world and everywhere you looked you saw strife. In Berlin you saw the barbed wire separating the two parts of the city. You saw strife in the Congo, and in almost every other part of Africa. You saw it in Cuba. You saw it in that most ironic place of all, Israel and Jordan, where the Jews and the Arabs are in constant conflict with each other, and where the Holy City is cut in two by the two enemies. You saw it in New Orleans, you saw it in Pittsburgh, and when you finally got back to Boston, you saw it there. You might very well have said to yourself, The strife over, the battle done? It looks to me as if it had just begun.

This is what makes me ask the question, Is there any real relationship between Easter in the churches and Easter in the South Pacific? Are we Christians, as we celebrate the victory of Christ on Easter Day, hypocrites, saying something we do not mean? Are we traditionalists who have been so long accustomed to the spring Festival of Resurrection that we cannot break away from it? Are we sentimentalists indulging in our emotions and feelings, enjoying the sensation of a victory that has no real meaning? Are we escapists trying to flee from the realities that actually exist in the world? Or, are we doing something on Easter that is really relevant to the world we live in?

I do not know whether you feel this question as poignantly as I do, but I feel it more keenly than ever before. It seems as though I am sometimes haunted by the possible incongruity between what we say, do, and feel in church on an Easter Day, when the air is vibrant with victory and alleluias, and what we know is going on in the world around us. It is to this question, therefore, that I wish to speak now, knowing in advance that I cannot and will not say all that can be said in answer to it, but saying only as much as I can say without the slightest reservation.

One thing we can say quite honestly is that the Easter victory has real relevance to us as individuals. In a way of speaking, we live two lives. One is private and the other is public; one is the life we live as members of a community, a society, a nation and a world; and the other is the private life that goes on within our own homes, and even more privately and secretly, within our own souls, and which often no one but God knows anything about.

We are something like passengers on a ship at sea. We are all on the same ship, we take part in the life of the ship, and what happens on the ship happens to us. If the seas are rough and the ship begins to roll, we roll with it. If the seas are calm and the sky is sunny and the ship is steady, we too are steady as we walk the deck. But in our cabins we are alone with our fears and our failures, with our joys and our victories, with our resources or lack of them, with our separate and various destinations in our minds, with our hopes for the future, our dreams and our prayers.

Most of us on a ship are not directly responsible for the sailing of the ship, but we are responsible for the way we handle ourselves on the ship, and what we are when we are alone in our cabins will at least partly determine how we meet things that happen on the ship, to the ship.

You see the meaning of this little parable without my interpreting it. We are living in a world that is going through one of the most severe storms in its history. (It has not yet really hit us here in the U.S.A. I have a feeling that before we are through it will, but it hasn't yet; it has only brushed our shores.) We know, however, that the storm is raging, and from time to time we can feel the ship rolling from side to side, and we get a sinking feeling inside ourselves.

We have no choice about this, and most of us cannot do much about the sailing of the Ship of State. It goes without saying that we can and must assume our responsibilities as citizens and voters, that is, as people who have opinions and who express them. All this I am not minimizing. But so far as the ultimate decisions go, most of us have very little to do with them. Nevertheless, we have to live through this storm, we have to live in our own private cabins as well as on the deck. All the time the storm is raging on the high seas, we have our own little battles to fight and our own fears and anxieties to handle and manage. We have our own attitudes to set straight, our own aches and pains to deal with, our own family problems to solve and our personal snarls to unravel and straighten out.

It is when we are alone in our cabins that Christ begins to have relevance to us as individuals, when we begin to wonder who we are, why we are here, and how we are going to carry on. He, too, knew something about storms. People thought that he could stop them, but there was one he could not stop, and that was the one that swept him away. That one he did not attempt to stop. He rode it out, and after it was all over, there he was, scarred, yet unscathed! Dead, yet alive!

This is the victory we celebrate on Easter, and we celebrate it honestly, at least as individuals, because we know that since that time he has steadied many a person through many a storm. He has saved many a person from making a fool of himself, and many others from hopeless situations of bitterness and remorse. Two people, whom I do not know personally, wrote me that as a result of a Good Friday service, they were reconciled to two people with whom they had been at odds for years. They knew the relevance of Christ to their individual lives.

He has steadied many a person through many a storm, and saved him from being inwardly destroyed by the rough seas through which he was sailing. He has given people a compass to steer by, and a port to head toward.

To us as individuals the victory of Christ, the fact that Christ is alive as a power in the world, has immense significance, because it helps us to handle our own private battle with the circumstances of life which are so often hard and difficult.

Granted that the Easter victory may be relevant to us as individuals, what about the world? We still have not answered that question. Has it made any difference at all to the world? Suppose you could get into outer space and look at the world from an objective point of view. Would it look any different now than it did two thousand years ago? Would it appear to have made any real advance in the conquest of evil? I am afraid that from an objective point of view the answer would be no. The world was in the grip of evil then, and it is in the grip of evil now. And yet, I cannot give a purely objective answer to such a question. I cannot honestly say that the answer is no, simply no, and for this reason, which may not appeal to you, but which makes all the difference in the world to me. Let me be specific about it.

On the same day that nuclear testing began in the South

Pacific, a man died in Cambridge, Massachusetts. He was ninety-two years old. His name was Henry Bradford Washburn. He lived a life of unbroken usefulness and service. He was a teacher of ecclesiastical history for thirty-two years in the Episcopal Theological School, and Dean of that school for twenty years. He was a man of extraordinary gifts who knew how to use what he had been given, and he spent himself lavishly. He went through more than one storm himself, some private ones about which we know a little, and many more that we know nothing about; and some public ones, two world wars and a major depression. In a world that is often stupid, he was always intelligent; in a world that is often cruel, he was always kind; in a world that has often lost its faith, his faith never wavered. He was a man of conviction, with loyalty minus animosity.

I speak of him because I knew him, and I felt the impact of his strong life upon mine. But there have been thousands of others like him during the years, thousands whose names are not known, who have left no mark in human history, but whose lives have been gathered together in the Society of the Redeemed, if we can use that theological phrase. They are those who have lived under the influence of Christ Jesus. Into the stormy seas of life these men and women have plunged, and I, for one, cannot believe that the winds and the waves have not to some degree at least been quieted by their heroic lives.

To come back to the very complicated and controversial question of nuclear testing, some think we ought to do it, and some think we ought not to do it; there are things to be said on both sides. There are very few, it is interesting to note, who think that we can do it with an easy conscience, and still fewer who are unaware of the tremendous responsibility we are assuming as we begin these tests. This represents moral and spiritual growth, and this I choose to think, is in part due — not entirely, but in part — to the influence of the Risen Christ upon the world we live in.

There is still something more to be said, however, for what happened on Easter *in* the world and *to* the world is *above* and *beyond* the world. Let me put it this way. When something is done that is ultimately true or good or beautiful, or more likely all three, it is done regardless of what the world thinks about it or says about it. The world can take it or leave it, respond to it or reject it, but it is done and it stands on its own right through all eternity.

Mathematics and physics are a closed book to me, but I have the imagination to know that when Albert Einstein finally, after years of work and experimentation, announced his equation that energy equals mass times the square of the speed of light, something was done; something was done *in* the world, yet regardless of the world. The ignorant people in the world could ignore it, the learned people could argue about it, but there it stood, in all its mathematical majesty. It was done, and in the long run all mathematicians and all physicists must come to terms with it.

In a different realm in which I am more at home, when Michaelangelo chipped out of that unlikely block of marble that had been discarded by another artist the figure of David, with scorn for Goliath in his stony eyes — it is unbelievable until you see it — with all the flexibility of youth and the strength of maturity in his graceful body, it was done. The people of Florence could put it outdoors and let the storms beat upon it, or later they could put it in a room where it stands now in its sublime, solitary beauty. But it was done.

In another realm in which we are all more or less at home, when Abraham Lincoln said, "With malice toward none, with charity for all," and when he confirmed those words by his life, something was done. The resentment of the North or the South, the conflict that followed after, have never touched what he said and did. It was something done, and it was something that judges everything else that this country will do so long as it endures.

Just one more illustration of what I mean because it points to something still further. When the young Ann Sullivan went down to Alabama and broke through the iron curtain of darkness and silence that separated Helen Keller from the rest of the world, it was something done, once and for all. Ever since then others have entered into it, participated in it, been inspired by it, shared the victory of it. Blindness and deafness still persist but they have been conquered, once and for all, and thousands have shared in that victory.

In somewhat the same way, although of course in a far greater way because these analogies are always less than the thing we are talking about, when God raised Jesus from the dead, it was something done, regardless of the world. The world could take it or leave it, but the miracle is that some people ever since have entered into it, participated in it, shared in its life. St. John caught this when in his Gospel Christ says, "Because I live, you shall live also."

So I can say, and I hope that you can say it with me as
we face together the ironies and contradictions in which
our world is enmeshed, because he did what he did, I can
do what I have to do. Praise God!

X

He *ascended into heaven*

IN THE SEVENTH CHAPTER we tried to see and feel what
happened when Jesus was crucified, and that was not a very
difficult thing to do. For one thing, all four Gospels describe the event in enormous and vivid detail. Also, it has
to do with things that we know about, things like sin, suffering, and death; cruelty, injustice, love, and forgiveness.
These things come close to the life we live, and touch the
most sensitive chords in our nature. Even an unbeliever at
a time like that might very well feel the power of the
Young Man, unjustly condemned, yet not condemning.

Then in the next chapter we tried to see and feel what
happened when Jesus rose from the dead. This took a little
more imagination. In this case, the accounts are extremely
brief and often conflicting. Also, the subject matter is
entirely outside the orbit of our ordinary experience. We
have all seen a man die; we have never seen a man rise from
the dead. Yet in spite of these difficulties, we know that
life often rises most majestically out of that which appears
to be nothing but dead ash. And if we have ever felt the
presence of the living Christ, his resurrection is no ulti-

mate obstacle to us as we try to enter into the depths of its meaning.

Now we come to the Ascension of Jesus. We want to see and feel what it means, and this takes even more imagination. To begin with, only one book of the New Testament tells the story in any detail at all, and that is the Acts of the Apostles, written by St. Luke. He tells the story that you have heard many times. Briefly this is it. Forty days after Jesus rose from the dead he was talking with his disciples on the Mount of Olives, and when he had finished a cloud took him out of their sight and carried him up into heaven. As they stood there gazing into heaven, an angel asked them why they were so amazed and told them that Jesus would come back the same way he had gone.

St. John and St. Paul refer to the Ascension, but only in passing. St. Matthew never mentions it, and when St. Luke tells the story in his own Gospel, he tells it quite differently. I wonder if you realize that in St. Luke's Gospel the Resurrection and the Ascension take place on the very same day, and that in the early manuscripts of the Gospel it is described in this simple sentence: "While he blessed them, he was parted from them." Also, the fact that a human being rose into the sky is not only a difficult thing for us to imagine and picture, but for many of us it would not mean much religiously even if we could picture it.

Yet the picture of Jesus ascending into heaven and sitting on the right hand of God has been carefully kept and closely guarded by the Christian community all through these centuries. It is one of the articles of faith in the Apostles' Creed; it has been preached and taught as part of the Christian faith, and the day has been celebrated year after year. We often wonder why. The answer is that the picture of Jesus ascending into heaven says something about Jesus that Christians believe and can say in no other way; no other way, that is, which can be easily and quickly communicated to the ignorant as well as to the learned.

What I should like to do is to point to a few of the things that the picture says, realizing that we cannot include everything. I have chosen three of the things it says which to my mind are particularly important.

The first thing it says is that Jesus, once rejected by men, now reigns in glory! Men and women, as you know, have a way of rejecting the best there is. It happens over and over again. Why men do it is a mystery; that they do it is a simple fact. But the best there is has a strange way of rising from the dead, so to speak, and ascending into heaven. For example, on an entirely different plane, the music of Johann Sebastian Bach was virtually rejected by men. It was forgotten. It lay buried in a grave for one hundred years, until Mendelssohn raised it from the dead. Then it ascended into heaven in the sense that all music, whether it is anything like Bach's music or not, is in a sense under its judgment.

So Jesus, once rejected, once spit upon, mocked, crowned with a crown of thorns, nailed to a cross, sent back, men thought, into the ground where he might be plowed back into the earth and into oblivion — Jesus once rejected, now reigns in glory. And he reigns *everywhere*. He is in heaven, the picture says. Where is heaven? Heaven is where God is. Where is God? God is everywhere.

When we talk about the Ascension, and affirm our belief in it, we are saying that we believe that Jesus not only reigns, but that he reigns everywhere, even where he has never been heard of.

Again, in an entirely different realm, the law of gravity reigns everywhere, not only in the scientific centers where men understand it, but also here where probably very few of us really understand it, and in the jungles where no one understands it. But its reign is supreme and, in the long run, everyone on the earth must come to terms with it.

So Christians believe that the law of God's reconciling love in Christ reigns everywhere, whether men recognize it or not, whether they accept it or whether they reject it. He reigns supreme. He is the Way, the Truth, and the Life.

He reigns where there is no visible sign of his presence, no tangible evidence of his authority. He reigns in sick rooms where there seems to be nothing but pain and sorrow and agony. He reigns in mental hospitals where there seems to be nothing but derangement, where the whole human enterprise seems to be denied any significance at all because it is so twisted. He reigns even in the houses of prostitution and crime where goodness is almost unheard of.

How can this be? you ask. This is the answer. Like the sun, he can be shut out of a life, or a situation. But also like the sun, he continues to sustain even those who shut him out. You can see why the music on Ascension Day is so full of triumph and victory.

If you believe this, something tremendous happens to you. In your life, at the present moment, you may see no signs of the power or presence of Christ. But the truth of the Ascension is that whether you see it or feel it or not, he is there just the same. Your nervous system, your physical equipment, your moral will power, may shut him out the way men pull down the blinds and shut out the sun, but he continues to sustain even those from whose lives he is shut out.

Also, he reigns the way he lived, in simplicity, and humility, and love. His love is a peculiar mixture of tenderness and austerity. His humility is a marvelous blend of honesty and humor. And his simplicity is a mixture of reality and security. These are the things that are supreme. He reigns not in pomp. We have the pomp and the majesty and the glory of the music to give to him but, if he should come to us now, he would not come dressed in elaborate vestments, or with any show of pomp or power. He would come the way he always came, in simplicity, humility, and love. You can see, I am sure, that when we say we believe that he ascended into heaven, we are saying that we believe that these are the things that really make the world go around. You can see what gigantic things are involved in this faith if you take it seriously!

A Christian cannot prove, of course, that Jesus reigns supreme, any more than a musician can prove that Bach's music is supreme. All a musician can do is to say, Listen to the music! All a Christian can do is to say, Look at him; enter into his life; let his life be in you; and then make your judgment. This, then, is the first thing that Christians believe and want to say about Jesus. He was once rejected, and he now reigns.

Another thing that the picture of the Ascension says takes us into deeper waters. It says that while religion may begin with the satisfaction of our earthly needs, it leads inevitably toward something higher, toward the place where our needs are completely overshadowed by something infinitely greater. Let me try to explain what I mean.

Do you remember why the Prodigal Son left the far country and went home? It was not because he wanted to see his father. It was because he was hungry. He had no money and no food. He went home and his father met him on the level of those needs, and answered them. But what his father really wanted to give him was love, and the relationship between the son and the father would never be fulfilled until the son met the father not only on that earthly level of his human needs, but met him, so to speak, in the air, in the sky, on the level of his father's love for him and his love for his father.

When we are in need we turn to God instinctively. When we are sick, we turn to him and ask him for health. When we are guilty, we turn to him for forgiveness. When we are discouraged, depressed, and defeated, we turn to him and ask for whatever it is that will lift us up out of the depths. And God meets us on that level of our needs. He came among us as a Man who ministered to our needs, who healed our wounds and forgave our sins. He identified himself with our human condition. This is the mystery of the Incarnation, God stooped to the needs of men. But in the Ascension, God does not stoop. In Jesus he rises up above our earthly condition; he reigns in heaven where his thoughts are not always our thoughts, where his ways are not always our ways, and where his will is not always our will. He draws us up from a preoccupation with our own needs to something that will completely overshadow them, and which will end in adoration.

Let me give you another earthly illustration of what I mean. There was a woman who for many years had been a victim of drugs. When she began to emerge from the valley of darkness, she took up painting to help her, to divert her mind, so that she would have something to think about which would help her overcome the pernicious and debilitating habit. And it did help her enormously. But what happened was that she who took up painting to help herself found that eventually painting took her up to an entirely different level where the painting and the beauty that she saw completely overshadowed her own needs, and she began to pursue the painting not for her sake, but for its sake. Do you see the analogy? I am sure you do see it, but whether you can do it or not is a question, for it is difficult.

All of us are inclined to take up God to help us over the hurdles of life. Then God eventually takes us up into an entirely different realm, where he asks us not so much what we need, but what we will do for him. Jesus, the God Incarnate on earth, soothes our sorrows, heals our wounds, and drives away our fears, and nothing will ever change that. But Jesus in heaven cannot hold our hands when we are in trouble; he wants our hands to use in place of his own. Do you see how this raises religion to an entirely different realm, and how the Ascension of Jesus points toward a more adult religion than most of us now have?

One more thing it says which I think it says to the people of our generation even more vividly than it said it to the people in the first centuries of the Christian era. The picture of the Ascension says that we are not alone in space. You may remember that those are the words of Mr. Khrushchev who said them when he was complimenting Scott Carpenter on his three orbits around the world in outer space. He was speaking about space in a physical sense and what he obviously meant was that the Russian Titov was no longer alone in outer space, that there were two Americans at least who had been there also.

But even in this purely physical frame of reference, there is a deeper meaning for those who have the eyes to see it. There is something about outer space so foreign to anything that we know anything about, so alien to us, that it almost frightens us, but the fact that a human being has been there makes all the difference in the world.

We look out not only at outer space, but at the cosmos, so vast in time and space, and so mysterious. With us it is often as it was with Pascal in the seventeenth century. As he looked up at the sky at night, he said, "The silence of those infinite spaces terrifies me." When we think of what lies beyond this little island of life on which we now live in time and space, we are sometimes afraid. The silence, the darkness, the vastness terrifies us. Then we remember that Jesus went into those infinite spaces; that one like unto ourselves, but far greater, is there; and that the God who reigns in those mysterious and often frightening regions that lie beyond the fringe of our understanding is the same God who once walked the earth in Jesus, and who left his footprints along our human way.

When we say we believe that Jesus ascended into heaven and sitteth on the right hand of God the Father Almighty, we mean at least this; that he who was once rejected now reigns; that we are not alone in space; and that if we are ever to enter fully into his life, we must meet God not only on earth, where we need him, but in the heavens where he needs us and where we can adore him.

XI

HE *continues his ministry*

"AND WHEN THE DAY of Pentecost was fully come, they were all with one accord in one place." The people referred to in that simple statement were Jews who had been intimately associated with Jesus and who were convinced, in spite of all the evidence to the contrary, that he was the fulfillment of all their hopes and fears. There was only a handful of them. There were no religious or political leaders among them. In fact, as far as we know, there was not a single prominent name in the group. If there had been a *Who's Who in Palestine*, their names would not have been included. The vast majority of their own people thought that they were not only mistaken, but that they were dangerous. They were upsetting the traditions of their people; they were disturbing what little peace there was left.

We pause long enough to point out the fact, so well known yet so often forgotten, that most of the great advances in life have been made by small groups of people moved by great convictions to do great things. The first colony established in the Western Hemisphere was the one Christopher Columbus left behind him on the coast of Haiti. And do you know how many people there were in it?

Forty! Forty people began the life of the New World. The Mayflower Compact was signed by forty-one people. And when men began to fly like birds, it was one man alone who flew across the Atlantic from West to East and landed safely on the other side.

We are accustomed in our day to mass movements, and I am afraid that we will be more and more influenced by them. But the movements that have really stirred the world have been the movements of a few dedicated people, and sometimes it has been one single person who has started the ball rolling.

This small group of dedicated Jews was meeting to worship God in the afterglow of their memory of Jesus. The upper room in which they were gathered may very well have been the same upper room in which the disciples had their last supper with Jesus. If it was, you can imagine the associations with which it was crowded. Even if it was not, the memories would have been there. After Jesus had gone, all the things in his life that they had seen were sharpened because of what had taken place in the meantime, and the things they had taken for granted, or neglected, or missed altogether, were in one way or another brought back to them. When they met together you can see how their minds turned backward to those days which they had lived through, but which in retrospect were even more vivid than they had been at the time. Now they remembered every word he had said, and every single thing he had ever done, and they even thought that he would come back to do the things that he had not been able to do while he was alive. When or how, no one knew. Meanwhile there was nothing to do but wait.

There are still people who are sitting and waiting for something to happen. *Waiting for Godot* is a play you may remember. Godot, who is always coming but never arrives, is a parable of much of our contemporary life. There are some who are nostalgically waiting for "the good old days" to come back, and of course they never come. There are others who are waiting for the golden age of peace and prosperity to arrive and, likewise, it never arrives. The attitude of expectant waiting is good, but if it dulls the edge of action, it is bad. Sometimes when you are in a very difficult situation there is nothing that you can do at the moment but wait. But you have to be ready to act at a moment's notice, when the time comes, when the wind changes.

Also, it is worth noticing that they were meeting on the day of Pentecost. It was one of the great Jewish festivals. In the beginning it was a harvest festival of thanksgiving, but by the time our Lord lived it was the day when the Jews commemorated the giving of the Law to Moses on Mount Sinai. Again, it is worth pausing to point out that in the normal course of events, one thing grows out of another. There is no human life completely independent of all other human lives. One life grows out of two other human lives who have come together in love. No society rises entirely upon its own foundations, but grows, as ours did, out of another society. Our society grew out of an older one that was wrought out by the Anglo-Saxon people, to which there were many contributions made by the Greeks, the Romans, the French and the Germans. It stands now upon foundations that other people have laid.

So Christianity did not spring into existence full-blown.

This I should like to emphasize because it is not always appreciated. Our Christian moral law grows out of the Ten Commandments of Judaism. Our Christian ethical ideals and principles grow out of the eighth-century prophets of Judaism. Our spiritual meat and drink come right out of the Psalms. And our God, whom we believe is incarnate in Christ, is the God the Jews were the first to meet in the desert, on the mountain, and in their corporate life.

On the day of Pentecost, therefore, they were all with one accord in one place, waiting, as it were, for something to happen. And something totally unexpected did happen! As the story in Acts goes, "And suddenly there came a sound from heaven as of a rushing mighty wind, and it filled all the house where they were sitting. And there appeared unto them cloven tongues like as of fire, and it sat upon each of them. And they were all filled with the Holy Spirit."

Surely I need not tell you that this is not the language a man would use to tell another person how to get to Concord. This is the language a man would use to tell another man how it felt to be in love. In other words, this is the language of imagination. You can, I suppose, although I would be the last one able to do it, describe the ascent of an airplane in precise, scientific language. You could describe exactly what was happening to the plane as it rose in the air, meeting the resistance of the air, and finally conquering it. But when you try to describe what will happen to people when their spirits begin to rise, then you say, "They will mount up with wings as eagles." In most cases you do not have to point out that they do not have wings, and that they are not eagles.

If you had been in the Upper Room on that day, you would have heard no wind and seen no fire. No one's hair would have been singed, no head would have been scorched. You would, however, have seen something happen to a group of individuals. You would have seen them taken out of the nostalgic memories of the past, in which it was such a temptation for them to dwell. (You know what a temptation it is for you to dwell in the golden memories of days that have gone.) You would have seen them drawn out of their dreams of the future, which had as yet no reality in the present, and you would have seen them plunged into the present life of the world. You would have seen them almost blown out of the Upper Room, which was so safe, so secure, so surrounded by familiar associations, blown right out of that Upper Room into the hostile streets of Jerusalem. You would have seen a group of people given something to do, namely, to tell the people all about this Life. And you would have seen them given the power to do it, the power of the Holy Spirit.

Every once in a while people ask me to preach a sermon on the Holy Spirit. They say, What is the Holy Spirit? I sometimes correct them and say, The more proper way to put the question is, *Who* is the Holy Spirit? "The Holy Spirit," in the words of my great predecessor, Phillips Brooks, "is God continually in the midst of men and touching their daily lives. He is the God of continual contact with mankind." That comes from a sermon that Mr. Brooks preached on Whitsunday. I would put it this way: the Holy Spirit is God as we know him when he comes among us, and gets inside us, and uses us. There is the celestial God of the cosmos who somehow keeps in control all the stars of the Milky Way, and millions of others of which we have no knowledge at all. There is the God who walked the earth in Christ Jesus, and there is the Holy Spirit who sometimes gets inside these rather inhospitable temples of our bodies and gives us power to do things that are quite beyond our normal powers.

So he came down upon that little group of people who had gathered together in one place with one accord, and they became the Christian Church. It is a very moving story.

This happened a long time ago, however, and it is only natural that people with alert minds ask the question, Granted that it happened then, can it ever happen again? They say — and I am now trying to paraphrase the words of people who speak seriously, not light-heartedly — Isn't the Church like a man with his future behind him? Aren't the great days of the Church in the past? Isn't it living on the momentum of its past life, and isn't the momentum very rapidly running down? Others say, Aren't we living in a post-Christian age? After all, science has not only changed the way men live, but has changed completely the way they think and, therefore, we can never have anything like the Christian Church in the new world that is growing out of the old one.

I, for one, do not believe it. I know that it will never happen again in exactly the same way, that history never repeats itself, and that the present situation is entirely different from the one that existed almost two thousand years ago. But I believe that it can happen because I know that it has happened, that it does happen.

To take one dramatic example, it has happened in the city

of Coventry, England. A new cathedral has been built out of the ruins of the old one. It is not at all like the old cathedral, no more like it than the old Gothic cathedral was like its predecessor built some five hundred years earlier. It is a witness to the resurrection, for it was built as evidence that men are willing and able to forgive, and that the chief mission of Christianity in the world is the Ministry of Reconciliation, and that nothing will daunt it, nothing can bury it, nothing can ultimately stop it.

Its architect is Sir Basil Spence. You might like to know that he is a Christian, and also an Anglican. So many of our good contemporary artists are completely outside the Christian fellowship, but here is a man who is not. He is a devout Christian, a member of the Anglican Church. When a journalist interviewed him, he said, "All my life I had wanted to build a cathedral." And when the interviewer asked him whether he thought it was right to spend so much money on a cathedral when there were so many human needs in the world, he pointed out that the total cost of the cathedral, when everything had been finished, was less than the cost of one bomber. He went on to say, "You must remember that there are two kinds of hunger, and physical hunger is not necessarily the most important. There is a hunger of the soul and that lies at the root of the world's troubles. I believe that Coventry Cathedral can remind men of God and their hunger for him. If that can be put right, then the other hunger will be well on the road of being overcome."

So the cathedral was built, a contemporary building, yet in the context of the ruins of the old. You may not like it, it will not be familiar to you, but it has been built in the spirit of the age and will be judged by future generations on its own merit.

There is in the cathedral a Chapel of Unity, the marble floor of which was designed by one of Sweden's great artists, and the money for the floor was given by the Church of Sweden. In that chapel people of all denominations, all faiths, will meet to read the Word of God, to think, to talk, and to pray.

Also, on the staff of the cathedral there is a full-time industrial chaplain who spends his time not in the cathedral but in the factories where the people work, carrying the message of the cathedral to them there, ministering to them in any way he can, sometimes only by befriending them. He has several part-time colleagues.

There are provisions for drama in the cathedral, so that religious drama will be encouraged and presented and performed under the best possible circumstances. There are provisions for radio broadcasting and television in the crypt.

In other words, this cathedral is a new, bold, and daring attempt made by the power of the Spirit to continue Christ's ministry of reconciliation in the world. And to emphasize the word *reconciliation*, I shall tell you this. A party of young Germans offered to rebuild the bombed vestries beside the ruined sanctuary, making them into an International Center of Reconciliation, and the money for that restoration (10,000 pounds) came from West Germany.

I, therefore, believe that the days of the Church are not in the past. I believe that what happened on Pentecost can in different ways happen again, most likely in small groups where dedicated people are willing to be picked up, possessed, and used as instruments of the Spirit of God, willing to set aside some of their own pleasures and profits, so that they can be the instruments of his love and witnesses to his resurrected, reconciling power.

I believe that it happens from time to time in our own church. We do not all think exactly alike, and I hope we never shall. But there are times when we are in one place with one accord, that God, so to speak, comes down into our lives, and sends us out to carry the burden, to meet the difficulties, to forgive the offender, to rise above despair, to seek and to save the lost.

So we meet together regularly, waiting, expecting the Spirit of God to touch us, to lift us up, and lead us out of the church into the streets where men and women live, work, suffer, and die. There we will be the instruments of his reconciling power, and through us Jesus will continue his ministry to the world, a ministry begun so long ago, with no fanfare save the angelic choir which none but the shepherds heard, and which men were foolish enough to think was nailed to a tree, sealed by a stone in a tomb. It is not so, it is not so!